.... for
New Teachers

This accessible, engaging guide contains all the advice you need to get you through your teacher training and the first year of the job. Written by Sara Bubb, the new teacher 'agony aunt', it's peppered with illuminating anecdotes and authoritative advice that will prove vital to all new teachers, including sections on:

- choosing and getting on a training course;
- what you have to do to get qualified teacher status, including the skills tests;
- succeeding on the course – study skills, planning lessons, managing behaviour and being observed;
- making the most of induction;
- looking after yourself and managing your time.

Updated with all the latest information and advice, the new edition is an indispensable guide to success in training and induction, and takes new teachers stage-by-stage from training to tackling their first job. It looks in-depth at the job-hunting process, applications and interviews, ways to make the most of induction and methods for managing time.

Sara Bubb has an international reputation in the field of induction and trains a wide range of people throughout the country and at the Institute of Education, University of London, where she is a senior lecturer. She has written books and numerous papers and articles on induction, staff development, workload and performance management. She has been th............
Times Educational Supplement. www.s............

D1151550

the insider's guide for

NEW TEACHERS

Succeed in training and induction

Second edition

SARA BUBB

Routledge
Taylor & Francis Group

LONDON AND NEW YORK

First published 2010
by Routledge
2 Park Square, Milton Park, Abingdon, Oxon OX14 4RN

Simultaneously published in the USA and Canada
by Routledge
270 Madison Ave, New York, NY 10016

Routledge is an imprint of the Taylor & Francis Group, an informa business

© 2010 Sara Bubb

Typeset in Bembo by Wearset Ltd, Boldon, Tyne and Wear
Printed and bound in Great Britain by TJ International Ltd, Padstow, Cornwall

British Library Cataloguing in Publication Data
A catalogue record for this book is available from the British Library

Library of Congress Cataloging-in-Publication Data
Bubb, Sara.
The insider's guide for new teachers : succeed in training and induction
/ Sara Bubb. – 2nd ed.
p. cm.
1. First year teachers–Handbooks, manuals, etc. 2. Teacher orientation–
Handbooks, manuals, etc. 3. Teaching–Handbooks, manuals, etc. I. Title.
LB2844.1.N4B822 2010
371.1–dc22   2009007755

ISBN10: 0-415-49933-X (hbk)
ISBN10: 0-415-49932-1 (pbk)
ISBN10: 0-203-87516-8 (ebk)

ISBN13: 978-0-415-49933-0 (hbk)
ISBN13: 978-0-415-49932-3 (pbk)
ISBN13: 978-0-203-87516-2 (ebk)

Contents

Preface   vii
Acknowledgements   viii
List of abbreviations   ix

Part 1   Training   1

1. **Choosing a training course**   3
   Entry requirements 4; Primary or secondary? 4; Training
   routes 5; Financial and academic considerations 10; If you're
   qualified to teach in another country 11

2. **Getting on a training course**   14
   Application form 14; Interview 16; Checks 20

3. **What you have to do to get QTS**   25
   Standards 25; Skills tests 28

4. **On a training course**   40
   Study skills 40; Writing essays 42; Lesson planning 45;
   Marking 49; Managing behaviour 51; Learning from
   observing others 54; Being observed 56

5. **Looking after yourself**   61
   Stages you might go through 61; Looking after yourself 62;
   Looking after your voice 64; Managing your time 67

Part 2   Your first year   73

6. **Looking for a job**   75
   Which country? 75; Financial incentives 78; Types of school
   79; Supply teaching 82; Moving between primary,
   secondary and special 84; What sort of school will suit you?
   86; Where to look for a job 87

7. **Getting that job** 90
   Finding out more 90; Application form 92; Interviews 96;
   Contracts 101; Salary 104

8. **Life in school** 106
   Before you start 106; Your classroom 109; Planning 112;
   Parents 115; Reports 119

9. **Understanding induction** 122
   Differences between England, Scotland and Wales 122; The
   rules in England 124; Roles and responsibilities 128; The
   induction tutor 133

10. **Making the most of induction** 139
    Professional portfolio 139; Setting objectives 141; The
    individualised induction programme 143; Observing others
    148; Being observed 152; Half-termly reviews 156; Being
    assessed 157

    Bibliography 166

    Index 168

Preface

In my roles running courses, doing research and giving advice for new teachers at the *Times Educational Supplement*, I come across many beginning and newly qualified teachers (NQTs) throughout the country. I have found wide variations in how people are being treated and a general lack of clear understanding about statutory induction.

My aim in writing this book is to make new teachers' lives easier by providing clear explanations and advice. The book has two sections: the first on training and the second on your first year. I hope to help you choose and get on to the right course and so have successful training. Finding the right place for your first teaching job is crucial. I aim to help you right through the induction period: from the initial visit, to understanding the standards you have to meet, to setting objectives, to setting up an individualised induction programme, to recording progress and finally, to being assessed.

I have not attempted to offer detailed help with, for instance, how to organise a class outing. There are other excellent books that do this. My focus is specifically to help you succeed in your training and induction year so that you get off to a good start in what must be the best career in the world – teaching.

Acknowledgements

This book has been written as a practical guide for NQTs to help them in their training and induction year. As such, I would like to thank all the people who post on the *Times Educational Supplement* NQT forum, and who come to my courses, especially those in Lambeth and at the University of London Institute of Education. These teachers have been an inspiration and guide to me in writing what I hope is a very practical book.

My past and present PGCE students must also be acknowledged, because they have given me such insights into how people learn to be teachers. I hope this book will help them get a fair deal in their first year of teaching.

I have made every effort to acknowledge sources throughout the book and would like to thank all who have helped me.

Most of all, I must thank Paul, Julian, Miranda and Oliver for their encouragement and tolerance of me while I wrote this book.

Abbreviations

AB	Appropriate Body
AST	advanced skills teacher
CEDP	Career Entry and Development Profile
CPD	continuing professional development
CPS	common pay spine
CRB	Criminal Records Bureau
DCSF	Department for Children, Schools and Families
EAL	English as an additional language
EBITT	employment-based initial teacher training
EEA	European Economic Area
EPD	early professional development
GTC	General Teaching Council
GTCS	General Teaching Council of Scotland
GTP	Graduate Teacher Programme
GTTR	Graduate Teacher Training Registry
HEI	higher education institution
HMI	Her Majesty's Inspectorate
HoD	head of department
ICT	information and communications technology
IEP	individual education plan
ISCTIP	Independent Schools Council Teacher Induction Panel
ITT	initial teacher training
LA	local authority
MFL	modern foreign languages
MPS	main pay scale
MTL	Master's in Teaching and Learning
NC	national curriculum
NQT	newly qualified teacher
Ofsted	Office for Standards in Education
OHA	occupational health adviser
OTT	overseas-trained teacher

OTTP	overseas-trained teacher programme
PGCE	postgraduate certificate in education
PM	performance management
PPA	planning, preparation and assessment
QTS	qualified teacher status
RTP	registered teacher programme
SCITT	school-centred initial teacher training programme
SEN	special educational needs
SENCO	special educational needs coordinator
SMT	senior management team
TA	teaching assistant
TDA	Training and Development Agency for Schools
TES	*Times Educational Supplement*
TPS	teacher pay scale
TSN	Teacher Support Network
VA	voluntary aided
VC	voluntary controlled

Training

one

Choosing a training course

Entry requirements

Primary or secondary?

Training routes

Financial and academic considerations

If you're qualified to teach in another country

So you've decided to be a teacher. Great! Despite all the recruitment problems and the advertising to tempt you into the profession, choosing and getting on the right training course for you is not easy. Every year committed people get turned down. This chapter will give you information about entry requirements, all the numerous routes you can go down and their financial implications. It has tips on completing application forms and being successful at interview.

The Training and Development Agency for Schools (TDA) website or Teaching Information Line should be your first port of call (0845 6000991). The TDA runs taster courses around the country. Some of these are aimed at particular groups, such as people from minority ethnic groups. These are well worth going to because they give you detailed information about routes into teaching and the answers to questions that you hadn't even thought of. They organise meetings with teachers and time in schools, and enable you to meet people in the same boat.

Entry requirements

The entry requirements to get onto any teaching course are fixed, so you need to make sure you meet them before even thinking about applying. The basic qualifications you need to be eligible to apply for a teaching course are:

- GCSE at grade C or above in English and Mathematics – and Science for those who intend to train to teach pupils aged 3–11;
- a degree, except for people applying for undergraduate teacher training.

Many courses are over-subscribed, and every year lots of people who have expected to be on a training course by the following September are disappointed. Courses can set their own entry requirements that are higher than the TDA basic ones, such as 2.1 degrees. You can apply for a course before the results of a degree or a GCSE re-sit are known, but obviously people with the qualifications already will have an advantage.

You also have to meet suitability criteria, such as:

- having the intellectual and academic capabilities needed to meet the standards;
- possessing the appropriate qualities, attitudes and values expected of a teacher;
- being able to read effectively and communicate clearly and accurately in Standard English; and
- meeting the Secretary of State's requirements for health and physical capacity to teach.

    (Training and Development Agency for Schools, 2008a)

You will also need to have a Criminal Records Bureau enhanced disclosure check and/or any other appropriate background check.

Primary or secondary?

You have to train to teach two consecutive age groups:

- Ages 3–5 Foundation stage: nursery and reception
- Ages 5–7 Key stage 1: years 1–2

- Ages 7–9 Lower Key stage 2: years 3–4
- Ages 9–11 Upper Key stage 2: years 5–6
- Ages 11–14 Key stage 3: years 7–9
- Ages 14–16 Key stage 4: years 10–11
- Ages 16–19 Key stage 5: years 12–13.

The first decision to make is whether you want to go for primary or secondary teaching. The fundamental difference is that primary teachers teach the same class all subjects for the year, whereas secondary teachers teach one subject to many different classes and year groups. Looking at your qualifications may help you decide. Degrees in a national curriculum (NC) subject are preferred for primary postgraduate certificates in education (PGCE), but if yours isn't, it's not the end of the world – you'll just need to convince interviewers of its relevance. Primary courses favour applicants who have a good range of NC subjects at GCSE and A level.

Secondary courses like you to have a good degree in the subject you want to train in. Again, if things aren't that straightforward don't worry. You need to be at degree level in the subject you're getting qualified teacher status (QTS) in by the *end* of the course, so you have time to get more knowledge on board. So, if your degree is in Psychology but you want to teach Maths for instance, you will need to emphasise how much maths there was in your course (statistics, etc.) and how you have high grades in A level Maths.

You'll spend 24 weeks on teaching practice in school on a PGCE secondary course and 18 weeks of a PGCE primary. In any course you will have experience of teaching in two schools.

Training routes

Choosing the right route and course is essential. The TDA survey (Training and Development Agency for Schools, 2008b) of newly qualified teachers (NQTs) found that 85 per cent of primary and 86 per cent of secondary teachers thought that their training was good or very good. The rest were lukewarm. In fact, 2 per cent rated their training as poor. This is a small proportion and maybe they're the Moaning Myrtles for whom nothing can be good enough – but what if their courses really were that bad?

It's worrying that only 67 per cent of primary and 69 per cent of secondary teachers thought their courses prepared them in knowing how to establish and maintain a good standard of discipline. Only 43 per cent of primary teachers thought their courses helped them teach reading well. I know much of this comes with experience, but it is a fundamental necessity.

Have a look on the Performance Profiles area of the TDA website (www.dataprovision.tda.gov.uk) to find out more about the institution you are considering. Look at the number of places available. Some institutions have many places, such as St Martin's College and the Institute of Education in London. At the opposite end of the scale, school-centred initial teacher training programmes (SCITTs) often have fewer than 20 places. All training courses, including small employment-based ones, are inspected, which is an important piece of information to glean. Read reports at the Office for Standards in Education (Ofsted) website (www.ofsted.gov.uk) and look at their ratings from when they were inspected.

Many people start training courses, but how many end up teaching? The TDA's initial teacher training (ITT) performance profiles are well worth looking at for this sort of information. Not everyone gets QTS at the end of training. Maybe they dropped out, maybe they had to re-sit a teaching placement or maybe they failed. Courses vary in their degree of people dropping out: look at the performance tables and choose somewhere that has a good track record.

The route you take and the time it will take you to achieve QTS will depend on your circumstances. The QTS standards you have to meet are the same whichever route you choose to go through. There are three main routes to QTS (compared in Table 1.1):

- The undergraduate route – you combine subject studies with professional training over three or four years and get a BA (QTS) or a BEd.
- The postgraduate route – this is offered full-time for one year, part-time or through a flexible programme, and gives a PGCE with QTS, unless the PGCE is for the post-compulsory sector.
- Employment-based routes (England and Wales) – this includes the Graduate Teacher Programme (GTP), which is for people

	BEd or BA (QTS)	PGCE	GTP
Entry requirements	English and Maths GCSE C, plus science C for primary	Degree. English and Maths GCSE C, plus science C for primary	Degree. English and Maths GCSE C, plus Science C for primary
Apply through	UCAS	GTTR	EBITT
Time spent in school	32 weeks for four-year and 24 weeks for three-year courses	24 weeks for secondary and 18 weeks for primary	All
Bursary	None	£9,000 for Maths, RE, ICT, DT, MFL, Music, Science; £6,000 for all other secondary subjects; £4,000 for all primary	No, but paid an unqualified teacher salary (£15,113+) by school. School may get training and salary grant
Golden Hello after induction year	No	£5,000 for Maths and Science; £2,500 for ICT, MFL, DT, MFL, Music	No

Table 1.1 Comparing routes into teaching

with a degree, and the Registered Teacher Programme (RTP), which is small and for people without a degree but with two years of higher education. Both courses give QTS. However, at the time of writing, this route into teaching is not recognised in Scotland.

Undergraduate route

The BA (QTS) or a BEd is a teaching qualification and a degree, and takes three or four years. It's great for people who know that they really want to teach, but is a bit limiting as a degree if you go into another career. Having said that, a degree is a degree and you will study at a high level in your specialist subject. A constant irritation for people on undergraduate courses is that they aren't entitled to any training bursary such as their PGCE colleagues get – and yet arguably have shown more commitment to teaching by doing a degree in education. Nor can they get the Golden Hello, even if they teach a shortage subject. To choose a course, take a look at the UCAS website (www.ucas.co.uk), which holds information on all undergraduate courses available, but check out how they do on the TDA performance profiles too.

Postgraduate routes

PGCE

The PGCE is the most popular postgraduate route, with about 17,000 secondary and 8,500 primary places – and it's probably the safest in terms of ensuring that you get quality training. PGCE courses last for about 38 weeks and are based at a university, but involve a great deal of time in school, usually in blocks. Primary PGCEs spend at least 18 weeks in school, and secondary PGCEs at least 24 weeks – over half of the course. When at college, you'll spend your time learning in lectures, seminars, workshops and tutorials. The PGCE combines theory and practice in a way that your first degree may not have, and you will have written assignments to do as well as planning when you're in school.

If you aren't able to train full-time on a traditional postgraduate course you might be interested in a flexible programme. Courses have multiple start and finish dates. Some have modules that you can do in the evening or weekends via distance-learning packages, others have an intensive full-time programme over a short period of time. At the start of your training, your previous achievement and learning will be assessed. This will be used to design a training and assessment programme that meets your individual needs. During your training you will receive support and guidance on your progress from the higher education institution (HEI) and schools involved in your training.

You can apply for a place on a PGCE through the Graduate Teacher Training Registry (GTTR). The GTTR system is that you complete one form online and state your training course preferences. You can choose up to four courses, in order, but only two for primary. Your form is sent to your first choice institution, and if they reject you it gets sent to your second choice, and so on. It is not easy to get places on popular courses so it's best to apply early. The GTTR starts taking applications in September, but you need to apply by December to get your application sent to your first choice for primary courses. Applications are processed by the GTTR in date of receipt order and despatched to the institutions concerned on a weekly basis. You can see the progress of your application on the GTTR website (www.gttr.ac.uk).

School centred initial teacher training (SCITT) is run by groups of schools, with input from HEIs and local authorities (LAs). All courses lead to QTS upon successful completion and may also lead to a PGCE validated by a university. You will spend almost all your time in schools. There are a fair number of SCITTs, but each has only a small number of places.

Graduate Teacher Programme

The GTP is for people with a first degree who want to train on the job in England or Wales. It suits people who have already got a good amount of school experience, because it can take only one, two or three terms, depending on your needs. Entry to the GTP is highly competitive. First, you need to be employed as an unqualified teacher in a school. This means that you will have to pay tax on your salary, which will be at least £15,000. Then you apply to an employment-based initial teacher training provider (EBITT). There are about 100 of these throughout England – see the TDA website for the current list. Look at how many places they have and how many TDA salary grants (£14,200+) and training grants (£5,000+) they can award. Places and funding go to the strongest applicants in each of the priority categories:

- secondary shortage subjects – Mathematics, Science, modern foreign languages (MFL), ICT, Design and Technology and English;
- high-quality primary applications;
- applications in any subject or phase that make the teaching force more representative of society – for example, increasing men in primary teaching, teachers from minority ethnic groups and teachers with disabilities;
- high-quality secondary applications in any subject;
- applications to train people currently working as teaching assistants (TA).

So, if you have a degree in History and Spanish, you would stand a better chance of getting a place with funding if you applied to train to teach modern languages rather than History. If your school is happy, you can do the GTP without any TDA funding.

The snag with the GTP is that you have to start working in a school as a teacher before even applying. Also, at the time of writing, this route into teaching is not recognised in Scotland. Competition for places is very strong, and experiences have been mixed, with some people feeling they were left to sink or swim. At the end you'll just have QTS, not a PGCE, so there is a slightly lower status. On the positive side, you probably won't have to go to lectures or write essays.

Financial and academic considerations

You should consider the financial incentives when considering whether to do an undergraduate or postgraduate teacher training course, whether to go for primary or secondary and what subject to go for. There are three sorts of incentives:

1. the training bursary;
2. Golden Hellos;
3. credits at Master's level.

The training bursary

If you do a PGCE in England or Wales, you'll get one. The size of the bursary depends on the phase and subject you are training in: at the moment you get £9,000 for shortage secondary subjects, £6,000 for all other secondary subjects and £4,000 for primary. Your training institution pays this to you, usually from October in nine or ten instalments. People on the GTP have to be employed by a school and are paid on the unqualified-teacher six-point scale. All pay scales vary depending on whether the school is in inner, outer or on the fringe of London or elsewhere in England and Wales. If you're lucky, your school might get a contribution from the TDA to the training salary and about £5,000 to cover the costs of your training. However, because there is a limited budget, some people get only the training grant or not even that. People on undergraduate teacher training courses get no financial assistance.

Golden Hellos

The Golden Hello is a financial incentive for people who do PGCE secondary priority subjects. You claim the money during the year after you've successfully completed induction if you are still teaching that shortage subject in a maintained school for at least half of your timetable. So, it's not so much a 'hello' as a 'thanks for staying'! The size of the Golden Hello varies. At the moment, people who do Maths or Science PGCEs get £5,000, while £2,500 goes to those who teach modern languages, Design and Technology, Engineering, Manufacturing, Religious Education, or Music. The money is subject to tax and national insurance.

Credits at Master's level

Many PGCEs now carry credits at Master's level. This means that if successful you will have credits that add up to one-quarter or even one-third of an MA. This is a boon, especially with the government's desire for teaching to become a Master's-level profession. It's a considerable saving in terms of fees and time – most 30-credit modules take ten weeks of three-hour evening sessions. You'll need to check whether and how many credits the PGCE courses you are interested in carry – most have 60 but a few have 90. The credits have a shelf life of five years, so you'll need to do the other credits needed for the full MA soon after you begin teaching. The Master's of Teaching and Learning (MTL) is geared up for this. The GTP is not an academic award so it does not carry any Master's credits.

If you're qualified to teach in another country

If you qualified as a teacher in the European Economic Area (EEA) or Switzerland, you may be eligible for QTS without further assessment. You can contact the General Teaching Council (GTC) (www.gtce.org.uk), who will assess your qualifications and, if approved, award QTS.

If you are not a national of the EEA and are not otherwise entitled to work in the UK you will have to apply to be given new sponsored skilled worker status within the points-based system. Have a look at current information at the UK Border Agency (www.ukba.homeoffice.gov.uk). You need a sponsor, such as a school, and a certificate of sponsorship. You are allowed to teach for four years in England as an unqualified teacher. The four-year period starts from the first day you teach in a mainstream school in England and includes breaks in service.

Many overseas-trained teachers (OTTs) are understandably resentful when they realise that the qualification from their own country does not fully qualify them to teach in England. However, in my experience people become more effective teachers in English schools through gaining QTS, and it gives them a focus for their professional development, the possibility of passing the Threshold and moving on to the upper pay scale − and another qualification for their CV.

There is much more to getting QTS than being a good teacher. It can be a long process unless you know the system. You need to apply for a place on the overseas-trained teacher programme (OTTP) to enable you to achieve QTS while being employed as a teacher. Contact your local EBITT providers. They are given an annual allocation of OTTP places and take responsibility for designing and delivering your training programme. For contact details, see the TDA website at www.tda.gov.uk/ebr.

Your qualifications will be checked. You will need:

- an overseas teaching qualification;
- a qualification equivalent to a UK Bachelor's degree;
- a qualification equivalent to GCSE grade C or above in Mathematics and English;
- a qualification equivalent to GCSE grade C or above in Science if you are applying for primary teaching.

The National Academic Recognition Information Centre (www. naric.org.uk) can provide information on the comparability of qualifications. You also need to demonstrate a good level of spoken and written English.

Once on the OTTP, you'll have a training plan set up to help you meet all the standards, including the skills tests in English, maths and ICT. The programme can take up to one year, but normally takes much less time. You can opt to be assessed for exemption from induction at the same time as for QTS, if you have quite a lot of teaching experience in this country or elsewhere.

two

Getting on a training course

- Application form
- Interview
- Checks

Application form

As soon as you've decided what route you want to go down and which course to apply for, you need to sit down with the application form. Some institutions get more than ten applications for every place they have, so they weed many people out from their application form. Yours needs to be good. You'll need some recent experience with children and young people in a school setting, not only so that you can write about this in your application and talk about it at interview, but to make sure that you really want to be a teacher. Consider one week's experience a bare minimum – the more the better.

Here are some tips for the form:

- Read through it to see the information it requires.
- Check the closing date and make sure you have plenty of time to contact referees, draft the form, write the personal statement, complete the form, check it and submit it online or post it.
- How many referees does it ask for? Normally you need to name two. Choose people who can say good things about your academic work and any experience working in schools or, failing that, with young people. Remember to ask people

if it is okay for you to put their names as referees and let them know timeframes.

- List your work experience clearly (the most recent first), emphasising things that are related to teaching. Follow any instructions about sending proof of qualifications and dead-lines. The institutions will stick to these.
- Write down all your qualifications, dates and grades. Be strategic: even if you failed GCSE biology, at least it will be useful to know that you studied it until you were 16.
- If you have yet to take or get the results of any qualifications, make this clear. This is particularly true for people retaking Maths, Science or English GCSE.
- Don't leave any box empty. For instance, people may assume that if you don't write in the grade of a degree that you have only a pass or a third.
- Write well and proofread – don't make any errors.

Your personal statement

Your personal statement needs to say why you want to be a teacher and why you should be given a place on the course. The reader will have to decide whether your application merits you being interviewed. You have limited space to write, so you'll need to plan what you say with great care so that you cover all the main points. Remember that the reader wants to be able to tell that you:

- will be able to meet the QTS standards – so they'll choose people who are well on the way to doing so, especially in terms of subject knowledge. A broad range of NC subjects at GCSE and A level will go some way to compensating for a non-NC degree subject;
- have the personal and intellectual capacity to be a teacher – you need to show intelligence and that you get on well with adults and children;
- can read effectively – so do everything the application instructions require;
- can communicate clearly and accurately in spoken English – take great care with your grammar and spelling, and construct

your writing concisely and as well as possible. I cannot tell you how many appalling howlers or how much illegible handwriting I have come across. Do not fall at this first and very straightforward fence;

- are committed to working with young people, particularly as a teacher – the role of a play-scheme worker is different to that of a teacher;
- have a good understanding of what teaching in schools involves – say exactly what recent experience you have had in schools and, if necessary, what you have arranged to have. If this isn't evident somewhere in the form you will probably be rejected;
- are committed to doing a teaching course – there is a high drop-out rate, so the person sifting through the applications will be looking for evidence of enthusiasm and staying power.

You also want your personal statement to be personal. Avoid blanket assertions, but give examples of what you've done, especially in schools: 'Observing in two schools has broadened my understanding of the importance of thorough planning to meet the needs of all children – and the time and expertise that this requires.'

When structuring your writing, think of how to be helpful to the reader. Express yourself with care. Address any problematic issues such as poor qualifications or gaps in employment that the reader is likely to have picked up on in other parts of the application form. Try to turn things to your advantage.

Finally, keep a copy and read it again just before your interview. Try to get into a school so that you can speak about a recent experience at the interview. You'll only get about two weeks' notice of the interview, which will probably last half a day.

Interview

You've been offered an interview – how exciting, but how terrifying! Again, preparation will be the key. Plan your journey with care, leaving room for the unexpected. There's nothing that looks as bad as being late for an interview.

What to wear? You've got to feel good and look the part. Your appearance will have an effect, possibly sub-conscious and therefore all the more powerful. Research shows that the content of what you say is only part of the impact that you make on interviewers. Voice and appearance matter hugely. Wear smart clothes, but make sure you'll be comfortable. Shoes can be a real problem if you're on your feet all day. A reasonably conservative look is safest. Smell is important too – don't turn up reeking of cigarettes or strong scent. Have emergency paracetamol, tissues and mints. If you're wearing tights, pack a spare pair. Eat breakfast. Turn off your mobile phone. There is nothing worse than a rumbling belly or a jolly ring-tone when you're in a room with strangers you're trying to impress.

Take a file with the copy of your application form, the prospectus, the letter detailing the interview schedule and a copy of an education paper to read while waiting. It will look professional and may come in handy in answering a question or two.

Possible interview formats

Interviews vary in how they are structured and how long they last. Ask when you accept the interview, if the information isn't outlined in the letter. Organisations will try to use a wide range of tools to identify the best applicants, looking for both academic and other skills, such as empathy, communication and resilience. Here is one interview structure, where each activity takes up to half an hour.

1. Introductory talk about the course. The opportunity for questions is available. Ask something that makes you stand out as keen and intelligent, such as the employment rate of trainees, when reading lists will be available or the library opening hours.
2. Group activity such as watching footage of part of a lesson which you then discuss, with someone watching and assessing you. This will be assessing your reflective nature and your interpersonal skills, so don't dominate or be a wall flower. Remember your body language.
3. An individual test – perhaps interpreting some data or correcting a badly written letter.
4. Individual interview.

What are your interviewers looking for? Commitment; a realistic understanding of what teaching is like; the ability cope with pressure; someone who acts, dresses and speaks professionally; someone who is going to be successful on the course, i.e. can write well, is punctual, appears to like children, is intelligent, can work in a team, has good subject knowledge and takes care with presentation. That's all!

> Q: I've been asked to give a five-minute presentation on an activity carried out within a school environment. What shall I do?
>
> A: Talk about some teaching and learning that you have seen, what you liked about it, what the children learned (focus on one or two), and what the teacher did to make it happen. If you haven't been in a class recently, get into one quick – you can't do it without this. In the presentation be lively, engage your audience, have some visual aids (children's work) and, most of all, come across as reflective. Could the children have learned more? How could the teacher have done it even better (but don't come across as overly critical)? Plan and rehearse it well so that you keep to time.

Interview tips

Relax. I know it's hard, but breathe deeply, wriggle your toes or do whatever works for you. Make eye contact with whoever is asking you a question. Be enthusiastic. Consider questions before answering and don't be frightened of a few seconds of silence – it's better than gabbling nervously and it shows that you are reflective, which is a highly valued characteristic in teaching. If you're stumped on a question, smile and ask them to repeat it.

You're likely to be asked questions along these lines:

- Why do you want a place on this course and for this phase?
- Why have you chosen this subject/age phase?
- What are the current issues in (e.g. geography) education and teaching?
- Why is your subject (e.g. history) important?

- Justify the relevance of your degree to the teaching you'll be doing.
- What makes a good classroom?
- How would you handle some difficult behaviour?
- Describe how you would spend a typical day if you were a teacher.
- How would you ensure that all children were treated equally in your class? Bear in mind gender, race, academic ability and language acquisition.
- What role should parents play in education?
- How will you exploit opportunities for literacy and numeracy in your subject?
- What areas of subject knowledge are you weaker on and how do you plan to remedy them?
- Tell us about a current educational issue and your view on it.
- What do you think the most challenging part of the course will be?
- What skills will you bring to teaching?
- What experience have you had that could help in your teaching career?

Answers to the hardest question of all, 'Why do you want to be a teacher?', might include one or more of the following:

- A teacher inspired me when I was a child.
- It's fun, varied. I'll never look at the clock.
- I like children.
- I want to do a worthwhile job.
- I like the creativity.
- I love my subject and want to pass on my passion.
- I want to give something back to society.
- I enjoy acting.
- Teaching is a career that values professional development.
- I won't just be making money for someone else.

Or maybe you don't feel any of these, in which case maybe you should try another career! Don't say 'the holidays'.

Justifying your degree can be hard, even when it should be easy. For instance, your English Literature degree will be relevant to your work as a primary school teacher because, er.... What do you think of these reasons?

> English is the medium by which almost all learning takes place, so children need good levels of literacy to help them learn in all subjects. The knowledge gained in my degree will therefore be used throughout the curriculum, but it will be of particular use in teaching literacy. I am very widely read. This will be useful in choosing texts. I can analyse texts well and have a deep understanding of terms such as metaphor, homophone and alliteration. I write and speak well, and can explain how different uses of grammar affect meaning, for instance. Perhaps most importantly, I have a love of stories, plays and poetry that I hope to convey to the children, and which will turn them into avid readers and keen writers.

You will be asked if you have any questions. You have, because you want to come across as an intelligent person who is highly committed. How about drop-out rate or employment chances from the course?

Checks

As soon as you're offered a place on a teaching course you'll be asked to complete a form about your physical and mental health and a declaration of any criminal history. These can feel traumatic and intrusive, but are a necessary check to protect pupils.

Fitness to teach

Teaching is a demanding career, and teachers have a duty of care towards the pupils in their charge. Even those training to become teachers need a high standard of physical and mental fitness, which is why ITT providers are required to assess the physical and mental fitness of entrants. The TDA guidance states that they need to be sure that trainee teachers:

- have the health and well-being necessary to deal with specific types of teaching and associated duties (adjusted, as appropriate) they are engaged in;

- are able to communicate effectively with children, parents and colleagues;
- possess sound judgement and insight;
- remain alert at all times;
- can respond to pupils' needs rapidly and effectively;
- are able to manage classes;
- do not constitute any risk to the health, safety or well-being of children in their care.

(Training and Development Agency for Schools, 2007: p. 5)

It's useful to understand that teaching is legally defined as:

- planning and preparing lessons and courses for children;
- delivering lessons to children;
- assessing the development, progress and attainment of children;
- reporting on the development, progress and attainment of children.

This means that, for example, there should be no presumption that a teacher has to be able to lift heavy objects, swim, drive a car, deal with every child's physical needs or go on trips.

You will be expected to complete a Declaration of Health form in order to prove that you are physically and mentally fit. This is an entry requirement for all courses that lead to QTS. Obviously, you must be completely honest: like the declaration of any criminal background, little will look worse than being dishonest. The form asks for your height, weight and information about eyesight, hearing and whether you smoke. It has a list of queries regarding major and minor ailments, such as 'Have you ever had depression?', to which you have to write a 'yes' or a 'no', and then give details as required. It also asks, 'Are you at present taking any medicines, pills, tablets or injections?'. Be precise in all answers. The doctor may ask for more information or a report from your own GP or consultant. In a few cases, people are asked to attend a medical examination.

Your declaration of health is read and assessed by the medical adviser at your training institution. The adviser will put you into one of three categories:

a.   Those who are in good health or who have conditions that are not likely to interfere with efficiency in teaching.

b.   Those in good health but who suffer from conditions that may interfere to some extent with efficiency in teaching. This includes some disabled people who need reasonable adjustments to enable them to teach.

c.   Those whose condition makes them unfit to teach. Few people fit this category, and it's only used after thorough consultation.

   (Training and Development Agency for Schools, 2007: p. 6)

The case study illustrates how things work.

Case study: fitness to teach

A candidate applied for a place on a primary PGCE programme. She told the tutor at interview that she had had a short period of depression following the end of a relationship, but on her fitness questionnaire she disclosed a history of clinical depression. The provider's occupational health adviser (OHA) sought further information from the candidate's GP: whether the condition was temporary or likely to persist; how far the candidate's condition was treatable; whether any treatment had been prescribed, and if so, how far it had been successful in regulating the symptoms that were giving concern. The GP's report showed that the candidate had had an 18-month history of bi-polar affective disorder, with a significant number of episodes of excessive mood swings.

   The OHA considered particularly how far the candidate's bi-polar affective disorder and its effects might:

* affect the quality of her insights and her ability to make sound judgements;
* affect her ability to communicate effectively with children, parents and colleagues;
* pose a potential risk to the health, safety or well-being of children in her care.

The OHA also considered how far the candidate could be enabled, by reasonable adjustment, to meet the fitness criteria.

Here are two possible scenarios and the resulting outcomes, to illustrate how decisions are made.

Scenario 1

The GP reported that the candidate had been undergoing a variety of treatments to help her manage her condition for over a year, and that this had been successful in regulating her mood swings. The OHA therefore concluded that her behaviour would be unlikely to pose a potential risk to pupils, and that the candidate had every chance of meeting the QTS standards by the end of the programme. She therefore declared the candidate fit to teach and informed the provider of this decision. In her report to the provider, without disclosing the candidate's medical history, the OHA suggested that the provider should write to the candidate to inform her about the counselling and support services available to trainees.

Outcome: fit to teach

Scenario 2

The GP reported that the candidate had been offered a variety of treatments for bi-polar affective disorder, but had refused to accept them, and in his opinion, without such intervention, the candidate would continue to experience excessive mood swings. The OHA therefore concluded that the candidate's behaviour would be likely to pose a potential risk to the well-being of young pupils. She considered what adjustments the provider might make to minimise the potential risk – for example, ensuring that the trainee was supervised at all times, but concluded that this was not reasonable. The OHA talked to the candidate about ways of reducing the risk, such as, through medication or counselling. The candidate was adamant that she did not need treatment but the OHA decided that the candidate was unfit to teach because, without treatment, her condition was likely to affect the well-being of young pupils. She made it clear to the candidate that were she to consider treatment she would be pleased to look at a new fitness questionnaire as part of a future application.

Outcome: unfit to teach

Source: Training and Development Agency for Schools, 2007: p. 24.

Criminal Records Bureau

Everyone working in schools is subject to checks by the Criminal Records Bureau (CRB). When you apply to be a teacher you have to apply for an enhanced disclosure from the CRB. This is not only to check if a person has a criminal background that might prevent them from working with children, but it will also show spent and unspent convictions and all cautions and further, it will also include 'relevant non-conviction information' from police records. The CRB sends the disclosure in confidence to the prospective employer, who is obliged to treat it in strictest confidence, so don't worry about lots of people finding out about your past. For more information, go to www.crb.gov.uk.

As soon as you've been accepted for a teaching course you'll have to have an enhanced disclosure of all criminal offences, no matter how long ago. This can be uncomfortable:

> I have had a six-month conditional discharge for a minor shoplifting offence from ten years ago, when I was 18. I am ashamed and embarrassed by it. I've held a professional job in industry for five years. If I want to train as a teacher how would this conditional discharge affect my ability to get on a PGCE course? I had thought the discharge was exactly that – finished with. Do I have to declare it?

Those working with children are not covered by the Rehabilitation of Offenders Act, so you should declare any offence you've committed, however long ago and however small. A criminal record doesn't render anyone unemployable. What would be a far greater problem would be for you not to declare an offence. It will come to light when the CRB check is made. Then the issue will not be the conviction or the 'crime', but your failure to disclose it, thereby bringing into question your basic honesty.

Once you get on a course you will need to meet the standards for QTS. These are outlined in the next chapter.

three

What you have to do to get QTS

Standards

Skills tests

QTS enables you to teach in maintained schools. In order to gain QTS you have to meet the standards required by the Secretary of State for Education.

Standards

The standards for the award of QTS in England, which you can find at www.tda.gov.uk/qts, set out what you must know, understand and be able to do to become a teacher. They apply to all trainee teachers in England, whatever route or course they're on. People training in other parts of the UK have to meet different standards – have a look at the relevant country's GTC website. For instance, the Northern Ireland competences recognise that each standard is a continuum to be met to different degrees, depending on a teacher's role, experience and context.

England's 33 QTS standards are arranged in three interrelated sections:

1. Professional attributes.
2. Professional knowledge and understanding.
3. Professional skills.

Your training institution will probably want you to track your progress towards the standards. Each standard has a rationale, detail relating to the scope of what is required, some key questions and links to other standards.

Unpacking a standard for QTS

QTS standard 1: Have high expectations of children and young people, including a commitment to ensuring that they can achieve their full educational potential and to establishing fair, respectful, trusting, supportive and constructive relationships with them.

Rationale

Education is part of the process through which people acquire values and learn to apply those values in the attitudes they adopt and the ways they behave. Teachers recognise the role they play in this process and demonstrate appropriate values, including a professional commitment to raising the educational achievement of all learners. Children and young people are more likely to thrive if they feel that they are valued and are confident that their teachers and their peers will support them. They are more likely to behave in a positive and constructive manner, and adopt appropriate values and attitudes, when they encounter such behaviours, values and attitudes in their teachers.

Scope

This standard requires trainees to demonstrate that they can help children and young people to achieve by establishing fair, respectful, trusting, supportive and constructive professional relationships with them, and by maintaining high expectations. They will need to demonstrate that they can create a purposeful and safe atmosphere characterised by respect and cooperation.

Questions

- Do you plan work at a suitably high level in relation to age and ability and to external benchmarks such as NC level descriptors?
- Do you plan to meet diverse needs?
- Do you encourage children and young people to contribute views and to reflect on, evaluate and learn from their mistakes?

> • Do you resolve conflicts and learners' problems sensitively to protect the self-esteem of children and young people?
> • Do you succeed in teaching children and young people to cooperate, to collaborate and to listen to others?
> • Do you build the confidence and self-esteem of children and young people?
> • Do children and young people show respect and sensitivity in their relationships with one another and in their responses to you?
>
> Training and Development Agency for Schools, 2008a

The evidence that you're meeting standards comes in three forms. The acronym DOD is useful to remember:

- Documentation: written evidence such as planning, assessment, marking, essays.
- Observation: observations of you in the classroom.
- Discussion: discussion with you and people who know your work.

People may be able to be accredited for their prior learning and experience. This may mean that there are parts of the course that you won't need to do in such depth, so you can spend more time addressing things that you're not so good at. Your trainers will be looking at whether you are well on the way to meeting any of the QTS standards before the course as a result of your experience. The difficulty lies in that there are gradations of meeting any criteria – you can always know more and do things even better.

If you feel that you have a great deal of learning and experience, you should get a folder and organise evidence such as your CV and job descriptions around each of the standards. For instance, standard 2 'demonstrate the positive values, attitudes and behaviour they expect from children and young people' is something you would consider you've done if you've worked as a classroom assistant. Evidence could come from citing some examples that could be backed up with the signature of someone who you've worked for. Think of all the little things you've done and the way you spoke that showed that you treat children with respect and consideration.

However, don't exaggerate what you know and can do – there's nothing to be gained. You want to be as good a teacher as you can by the end of your training, and repeating or going deeper into things can be really beneficial.

Skills tests

All trainee teachers must pass the skills tests in ICT, literacy and numeracy, irrespective of their qualifications, subject specialisation or age group taught. The skills tests were brought in 2001 amid great controversy. The reason for inventing them is 'to ensure everyone qualifying to teach has a good grounding in the use of numeracy, literacy and ICT in the wider context of their professional role as a teacher' (TDA website). Fine, but it's pretty insulting to think that these things wouldn't be picked up easily in the course of training by graduates who have to have Maths and English GCSE – and why have a test for these things? Would you ever have to work out this little gem from the mental arithmetic part of the numeracy test in test conditions?

> A teacher started an activity which lasted $1\frac{1}{4}$ hours at 13:35. What time did the activity finish?

Typical comments from people who have done them include:

> They were basic and easy to do, and the whole process was well organised, but they were hyped up to be a lot worse than they were. It was too much added stress for nothing.

> They are an extra hassle in an already horrifically busy schedule. The fact that we need GCSE English, Maths and Science to get on the course should be enough evidence without these tests.

> I passed the tests, but they were a waste of time. I should have been concentrating on my teaching practice.

Still, everyone needs to pass all three skills tests in order to get QTS. Don't allow yourself to worry about them until you've failed at least one, if not two, attempts. I know that's no comfort to those of you who go to pieces in tests; don't feel very confident at maths/literacy/ICT; aren't brilliant with computers, especially an unfamiliar one; and would prefer to be tested with a pencil and paper. But put them into perspective. Surely compared to teaching 30 children every day, they should be seen as a minor inconvenience? I hope this chapter will reassure you that they're perfectly do-able: to be forewarned is to be forearmed.

Registering and booking

When I said 'minor inconvenience' I was referring to the tests themselves. Registering and booking them have been challenges in themselves for many people. To register you will need the registration number issued by your ITT provider. Your unique registration number is linked to your ITT provider; you must enter the correct ITT provider name to ensure they are able to view your results. Once registered, you will receive your username and password within two working days. This will allow you to book the tests. All correspondence, including your username, password and test booking confirmations, will be sent via e-mail, so use a current e-mail address and keep checking it. To prevent e-mails going straight into your junk-mail box, add e-mail addresses into your address book. If you lose your registration number, you will need to ask your training provider, who will be able to check the number that was assigned to you.

If you have a disability such as dyslexia or a visual or hearing impairment, or if English is not your first language, you can apply for 25 per cent additional time in which to complete the test. This is well worth applying for, but can only be done at the time of registering. State whether you require any special arrangements.

There are test centres throughout England, only some of which are located within ITT providers. Each centre has between five and eight test machines, so bearing in mind that there are about 38,000 people trying to take them each year, you'll see that you need to get organised. Opening times vary. They are generally open for at least 18 hours per week, between the core hours of 9 a.m. and 4 p.m. Some are also open in the evenings and at the weekends. Test centres are normally open for longer periods during the busy months of October and November, and shorter periods during July and August, when demand is low.

If you find that you can't attend a test, cancel through the booking page. From here you can reschedule your tests. If you're unable to cancel your test in advance, for example, if you fall ill on the day of your test, please contact the helpdesk, who will advise the test centre on your behalf. The number of 'no-shows' are monitored and training providers will get told about persistent offenders!

Book the tests as soon as you can to allow time to re-sit if necessary before the end of your course. Details of directions, maps and general opening hours for each test centre are on the TDA website. You may as well book to take all three tests on the same day. The literacy and numeracy tests run for 45 and 48 minutes respectively, and the ICT test takes 35 minutes, so you need to make sure you leave some time for a brief breather between them, e.g. the numeracy test booked at 9.00 a.m.; ICT at 10.30 a.m.; and literacy at 11.30 a.m. Then lunch!

When you take the tests you must have two lots of proof of identity to show the test centre administrator. The primary ID must include your photograph, name and signature, such as a passport or driving licence card. The secondary ID must include your name and signature. The only equipment you'll need is a pen or pencil. Paper for rough working out and an on-screen calculator is provided for the numeracy test. You get your results at the end of the test.

Preparing

You need to prepare for the skills tests, as you would any other exam. I've known people who've come a cropper because they thought that because they had a degree in the subject that they would be okay. So some preparation is needed, but don't go overboard – you can take them as many times as you need and no-one will know that you didn't pass first time … unless you tell them. Support materials on the TDA website help you practise sample questions, test yourself, check your answers and consult the commentary provided on the questions. There are interactive and non-interactive practice tests. The benchmark tests are useful. They help you get a feel for the level of knowledge required to pass the

	Pass (%)	Pass at first try (%)	Pass at second try (%)	Mean number of attempts (%)
Numeracy	97.8	76.7	44.8	1.53
Literacy	98.9	82.0	60.4	1.35
ICT	99.4	90.5	77.5	1.08

Table 3.1 Skills tests pass rate 2006–07 (www.tda.gov.uk/skillstests)

tests. Look at the pass mark for these benchmark tests – at 60 per cent, they're not hard. There are also books on the market. Of vital importance is that you get used to working quickly, since the tests have a time limit. More information is available from the TDA website (www.tda.gov.uk/skillstests).

Most people say they find the ICT test easiest. This is reinforced by the statistics. Table 3.1 shows that although the overall pass rates are high, trainees often needed more attempts to pass numeracy than literacy or ICT. Undergraduate trainees needed slightly more attempts than postgraduates, and people training to teach the 3–8 age group took more attempts than those training to teach older primary pupils. People whose first language is not English needed more attempts in both tests than the average.

Numeracy test

Each numeracy test covers

1. Mental arithmetic (12 marks)
     This section will test your ability to carry out mental calculations using, for example, time, fractions, percentages, measurements and conversions.
2. Interpreting and using statistical information (7 marks)
     This section will test your ability to:
   - identify trends correctly;
   - make comparisons in order to draw conclusions; and
   - interpret information accurately.
3. Using and applying general arithmetic (9 marks)
     This section will test your ability to use and apply general arithmetic correctly using:

- time;
- money;
- proportion and ratio;
- percentages, fractions and decimals;
- measurements, e.g. distance, area;
- conversions, e.g. from one currency to another, from fractions to decimals or percentages;
- averages (including mean, median, mode and range where relevant);
- simple given formulae.

The content of the test is meant to be relevant to your professional role as a teacher, and the majority of questions are written using data commonly available within schools which an NQT could be expected to use. So it's things like national test data, progress attainment, special educational needs (SEN) ratios, subject choices, costings, budgets, mark schemes, timetabling and planning school trips. The total number of marks available in the numeracy test is 28. Each question carries one mark.

Most people find the mental arithmetic hardest, but again practise helps. On the mental maths, they read the question twice. Write the key numbers the first time and listen the second. You have to wear headphones and answer questions such as the ones below from the website (www.tda.gov.uk/skillstests).

Mental maths example

1. Twenty per cent of the pupils in a school with 315 pupils have free school meals. How many pupils is this?
2. The entrance fee for an exhibition is £3.75. What will be the total entrance fee for a school party of 50 pupils?
3. In a year group of 180 pupils, 5 per cent achieved below level 3 in English Key stage 4. How many pupils achieved level 3 or above?
4. A test had 40 questions, each worth one mark. If the pass mark is 60 per cent, what was the minimum number of questions that must be answered correctly in order to pass the test?
5. One gallon is approximately 4.5 litres. About how many litres is 200 gallons?

6. Two-fifths of a class of 25 pupils were girls. What percentage were boys?

7. A school had 1,200 pupils on roll. In the first two weeks of term, 90 per cent of the pupils used the school library. How many pupils did not use the school library in the first two weeks of term?

8. Three-eighths of a year group of 360 pupils were boys. How many of the group were girls?

9. In a class of 24 pupils, three-eighths are involved in a school concert. How many pupils are not involved in the school concert?

10. The science department in a school has an annual allowance of 600 reams of paper. 310 reams are used by December and a further 160 reams by March. How many reams are left?

11. It is possible to seat 40 people in a row across the hall. How many rows are needed to seat 432 people?

12. All 300 Year 11 pupils in a school took GCSE English. The number of pupils gaining grade C or above increased from 85 per cent in the mock exam to 93 per cent in the actual exam. How many more pupils gained grade C or above in the actual exam than in the mock exam?

13. A teacher is planning a group outing to see a play in a nearby city. The play begins at 3:30. It will take five minutes to walk from the city station to the theatre. To get their group seating the group needs to be at the theatre at least 15 minutes before the play begins. Click on the latest train departure time the group can take from the town to get to the theatre at least 15 minutes before the play begins.

Depart	Arrive
13:45	14:30
14:06	14:51
14:13	14:58
14:27	15:12
14:46	15:31

Literacy test

Each literacy test covers four areas:

- spelling (1 0 marks available);
- grammar (8–12 marks available);

- punctuation (15 marks available);
- comprehension (8–12 marks available).

Spelling must be attempted first, and then the other three sections may be attempted in any order. You're asked to write words that you hear, but they are put into the context of some sentences about school. The TDA chooses words that aren't unusual but which are a little tricky, such as procedural, ineffective, grammatically, independently, accommodation. In the punctuation test, the little hand turns grey when it is expecting you to insert a change. It won't let you put a piece of punctuation where none should be.

Example of the grammar test

Complete the following passage. Select the best of the given alternatives at the points at which there are blank lines. You will need to check that you have made the best overall set of choices for completing the passage.

This is part of a recommendation for a commendation certificate from a Class Tutor to a Head of Year.

Memo to: Head of Year
From: JG
Date: 21/6/00
Subject: Half-termly recommendations for my tutor group
I suggest Abdul Rashid for a commendation certificate. Abdul's successes this half-term include:

- being consistently on time for registration;
- completes homework and hands it in promptly;
- completing and handing in promptly his homework;
- completing homework and handing it in promptly;
- acting as homework monitor for Ms Saheed.

As monitor he also checked for latecomers and made sure that the last of the books was handed in.

In addition, Abdul has been responsible for helping the lunch time assistants.

Finally,

- having been very negative in the past, his change of attitude has been most encouraging this term.
- Abdul's attitude, having been very negative in the past, has been most encouraging this term.
- having been very negative in the past, Abdul has been most encouraging this term.
- his attitude has been most encouraging this term. Having been very negative in the past

Source: www.tda.gov.uk/skillstests.

Example of the punctuation test

Most of the original punctuation has been removed from the following passage.

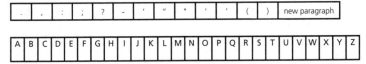

What should teachers and parents be aware of

The Internet is a reflection of the people who make up our society it is not controlled by any particular organisation and the standard or source of information cannot always be guaranteed. Individuals rights to freedom of speech and freedom of choice must be observed, but balanced against the rights of younger users although not common users will also wish to guard against the possibility of 'hacking' and computer viruses.

While schools and parents need to exercise caution in the access which they allow children to the Internet they should not be deterred from using it its educational benefits outweigh any possible dangers, which are comparatively minimal. Schools have always helped learners to engage with society through clear support and guidance, and use of the Internet should be no exception.

As with television and video parents carers and teachers should preview material or provide supervision, as well as having a more general strategy in place for ensuring childrens safe use of the Internet. These strategies can use a combination of measures

Source: www.tda.gov.uk/skillstests.

Example of the comprehension test

Read the following excerpt from the report on the Improving Primary Schools research project from the LA section of the DfES Standards web site and then answer the questions.

Aim

In the context of a large body of research about the factors which make schools effective, the LA wanted to look more closely at the process of managing change to effect improvement.

Improving primary schools in Hampshire were identified by using their end of key stage results The increase in average levels since 1995 for KS1 and 1996 for KS2 were used. Confirmation was given by the attached adviser/inspector that the improvements indicated by the data were the results of actions taken by the school.

The ten schools selected covered a wide range of size, type and location.

Each project headteacher was 'paired' with a colleague in another project school, usually a different type of school in another location. Each prepared a paper on what they had done to effect change in their own school. 'Research teams' comprising the paired heads and two LA adviser/inspectors made visits to each project school. Interviews with headteachers and observations took place in each school. School documentation was scrutinised and parents', pupils' and governors' views sought. The LA adviser/inspectors analysed the resulting data and identified the common factors of the improving schools which were then presented to the project headteachers for ratification.

The project appears to have elicited is a number of common factors which create the conditions for effective change leading to school improvement. The headteachers involved all found the experience to be a useful opportunity to reflect on practice.

The authority has already held two adviser/inspector sessions where the findings were shared and where they planned how to use them with the current work on school improvement across the service. Four county dissemination days are planned, which will include the headteachers from the project schools. The LA believes the case studies and research conclusions from the project will be valuable training tools which will also inform its ongoing work on school improvement. All schools will have copies of the project report and will be encouraged to use them for self-evaluation purposes.

Question

Matching texts to summaries
   Select the sentence which summarises paragraph 4 most effectively.

- Research teams inspected project schools and advisers and inspectors analysed results.
- Common factors were identified by inspectors and presented to heads for confirmation.
- Heads from the project schools were paired and worked on a report of their attempts to bring about improvements in their own schools.
- Pairs of heads and inspectors worked to identify common factors in schools which were improving.

Source: www.tda.gov.uk/skillstests.

ICT test

Each test contains five tasks and each of these tasks contains four sub-tasks. It covers the following types of software:

- presentation
- e-mail
- text editor
- spreadsheet
- browser.

It's a bit like testing you on everything in Microsoft Office, but with some irritating differences. The spreadsheet is like Excel but it doesn't have the handy icons. Instead, there are words that you have to scroll down. Just keep calm and work through slowly.

   The tasks can be completed in any order. When you are in the test, choose a task from the menu bar at the top of the screen. Look at the examples to see the sort of thing you're asked to do.

ICT test example 1: presentation

Launch the presentation software. Open the InternetResources presentation which is located in the School Network/Staff Training folder. Use the mastersslide setting to change the following:

- Set the title text to 32pt.
- Set the body text to 18pt.
- Change the background colour on all slides to red (4).
- Set the slide transition to Fade In, with a delay of 3 seconds for all slides.

Cut the image from the third slide and paste it in Slide 2. Your Headteacher has sent you an e-mail with an image attached. Save this attachment in the School Network/StaffTraining folder. Use the image as the replacement image for Slide 3. On Slide 4, change 'Need to make learning fun' to read 'Novelty makes learning fun'. Left align all the text on this slide.

Save the revised presentation as 'InternetResources2' in the School Network/StaffTraining folder. Print 3 copies of the presentation in Landscape Orientation on the Network Printer using the Best Quality option. Set up a reply to the Headteacher's e-mail. Attach a copy of the presentation. In the body of the e-mail, insert the text 'Image changed as asked. See attached.' Send the e-mail.

ICT test example 2: Ardean Hall

You have agreed to help with the finishing touches to a handout for the visit. To do this you need to:

a) locate a website and download a picture
b) add the picture and some formatting to the handout

Part 1.1 Locate the 'Ardean Hall' website by using the search option on the '24 Hour Museum' website. The 24 Hour Museum is connected to the NGfL website.
Part 1.2 Locate and download the picture of 'Ardean Hall'.
Part 1.3 Insert the picture file you have downloaded into the 'Handout' document below the heading 'View of the front of Ardean Hall'.

Part 1.4 Insert a copyright symbol before the words 'Ardean Hall 2001'.

Part 1.5 Add bullet points to the list of 'staff organising the visit'.

ICT test example 3: National Poetry Day

Your Head teacher has asked you to do some research in preparation for National Poetry Day. Click on the green Forward arrow above to start the task.

Task 1 As requested in the e-mail from your Headteacher, return to the Whadshire Local Authority website that was visited last week. Bookmark the page that lists the projects available; rename this bookmark as 'WhadshireProjects'. On the WhadshireProjects page click on the Adopt a Poet project. Follow the link to Bob Bramwell's site and bookmark his home page. Set up a reply to the Headteacher's e-mail. Include in the body of the e-mail the message 'We could book this poet for the day.' and the web address of Bob Bramwell's home page. Send the e-mail.

Task 2 Print Bob Bramell's Contacts webpage on the Admin printer using Draft Quality. Jane Braithwaite has asked you by e-mail to find a suitable logo for a poster promoting National Poetry Day. Review the InternetRules file in the School Network/Admin folder. Check the maximum file size allowed for downloading. Return to the Adopt a Poet page on the WhadshireProjects site and download a suitable image; save it in the School Network/PoetryDay folder.

Task 3 Set up a reply to Jane's e-mail. Attach the image you have chosen. In the body of the e-mail, insert the text 'Is this image okay for you?' Send the e-mail. Organise your bookmarks by setting up a folder called 'PoetryDay'. Move all bookmarks you have created today to this new folder.

Task 4 Check your work and then save any files that you have modified. Close all programs to complete the task.

The next chapter outlines other aspects of a training course.

four

On a training course

- Study skills
- Writing essays
- Lesson planning
- Marking
- Managing behaviour
- Learning from observing others
- Being observed

There is more to being on a teacher training course than meeting the standards. This chapter covers a few key aspects of life at college and in school that will help you succeed.

Study skills

People often assume that if you've got so far in the education system then you won't need study skills training, but this is a mistake. You're bound to be really busy on the course and improving study skills can help to boost your efficiency.

The first thing you need to do is to get organised physically, so find a space where you can be comfortable to work. Buy yourself some files and some stationery and do your best to get hold of a computer. Make a wall planner and draw up a timetable of when everything needs to be done by. Then work backwards from deadlines, setting yourself some smaller targets. Your college deadlines will have been well thought through by your course leader so that your considerable workload is spread over the duration of the course. If you stick to deadlines you'll be fine. If you break them, problems will snowball and you'll end up having to write essays when you should be preparing for teaching.

Think about when you work best and what use you can make of 'dead' time – time during which you could be doing something beneficial, such as reading on the bus. Get to the library before everyone else on the course borrows the most useful books. Work with friends to share books, articles and notes. Concentrate on reading the recommended texts rather than every single item on the library shelves, and try to target the most up-to-date materials. They usually summarise the best of what has been written before. The Internet has lots of good stuff on it, but eats up time. If you're like me, you'll get sidetracked. Be ruthless with your time and just go to recommended sites.

Diving into a book and working through to the end is usually unnecessary and wastes time. Be clear about what kind of information you want to find, and why. Look for relevant sections and make judicious use of the contents page, introduction and index. Scan headings and summaries. Skim read, so that you focus on the most useful parts of the work – the key points.

Making notes aids absorption and concentration and helps you summarise arguments, information and ideas. Spot and record key words or concepts. Mind maps are really useful. We quickly forget most of what we read, so put the book down and try to jot down key ideas. Don't take masses of notes or write lots of quotations. Summarise in your own words and jot down page numbers so you can reference ideas and go back to the book if necessary.

Get into the habit of checking through your notes – writing a summary sentence can be useful. Regular review of what you have read or heard in lectures stimulates understanding so your knowledge grows and becomes integrated with other information.

Academic referencing in essays can be tiresome if you haven't kept a list of everything you've read in the required format. So start a file of references in alphabetical order that you can cut and paste into an assignment at a later date. Check on the style that your course requires – this may not be what you're used to. Here's a standard way to reference sole-authored and multiple-authored books, academic journal articles, newspapers and websites:

Book
Bubb, S. (2007) *Successful Induction for New Teachers: A Guide for NQTs and Induction Tutors, Coordinators and Mentors.* London: Sage.

Article in a book
Bubb, S. and Earley, P. (2007) 'The school workforce in London' in Brighouse, T. and Fullick, L. (eds) *Education in a Global City: Essays on London.* London: Institute of Education, pp. 147–168.

Journal article
Bubb, S. (2008) 'CPD: so what?' *CPD Update*, May 2008, Issue 106, pp. 6–7.

Newspaper article
Bubb, S. (2009) 'More recruits equals extra competition for teachers' *The Independent, Education & Careers*, p. 8. 5 February 2009. www.independent.co.uk/student/career-planning/getting-job/more-recruits-equals-extra-competition-for-teachers-1545626.html (accessed 19 February 2009).

Research report
Bubb, S., Earley, P. and Hempel-Jorgensen, A. (2009) Staff Development Outcomes Study. London: TDA. www.tda.gov.uk/upload/resources/pdf/s/staff_development_outcomes_study.pdf (accessed 19 February 2009).

Writing essays

For those of you who've had a break from studying, one of your greatest challenges will be actually writing an essay.

> I am having a fairly nightmarish time. Finding my time management appalling and writing my first assignment well nigh impossible. I completely lack the power to edit down and be discriminating. I have read far too many essays in edited books and have lost the power to think and articulate for myself on the heady question of the literacy objectives.

This paralysis from reading too much is very common. What you need to do is to close all books and then consider what the question wants and what *you* think. Write down the points you want to make, then think of examples from your school experience and other people's views that you've read about. Put them into some logical order so that you develop an argument. In most PGCE essays, it's important for the reader to hear your voice (use 'I'). This may be quite different to the expectations of you as an undergraduate. Don't use jargon and buzz words for their own sake. Say what you mean.

Aim small: one paragraph at a time. Just write down your ideas and don't look back until you've finished a paragraph. Yes, it probably will look awful, but don't try to edit straight away. Leave it overnight and you may well be more impressed with yourself. Once you've written what you think needs to be said, you can whiz though putting in references. Don't use too many quotations, but do make sure that you can't be accused of plagiarism – your lecturers will be able to spot ideas and phrases that you've 'borrowed' without referencing.

Read the assessment criteria and aim to meet each at the highest level. Look at Table 4.1 to see what might be expected from an A-grade piece of work on a PGCE that carries Master's-level credits. Weave theory and practice together: 'The Code of Practice (DfES 2001) says ... about children with special needs. I consider these aims laudable but I have found teaching an autistic boy in the mainstream classroom very difficult.'

Leave the introduction and conclusion till last. They're the most important bits and, anyway, how do you know what you're going to say until you've finished it? No matter how well you plan, your work will evolve. Your introduction or abstract needs to guide the reader through your work, so define any terms you're using, describe the context of the school experience you're drawing on and briefly outline the structure of your writing. Conclusions are very hard. Sum up the key points you've made and perhaps try to end on a 'what else needs to be known' note.

Once you've finished, spend a good amount of time editing. Look at the assessment criteria and try to judge what you've written against them – could you do any better? Keep to the word limit, though going over by 10 per cent is usually acceptable. Cut out any waffle. Use the UK English grammar and spell-check

	Requirements for an A grade
Knowledge and understanding	Demonstrates excellent, systematic knowledge and understanding of teaching and learning and of professional practice within their field, phase or subject. Such knowledge is thoroughly informed by recent and relevant theory, research and evidence and a critical understanding of the significance, application and limitations of appropriate educational research.
Application of knowledge and understanding	Offers a comprehensive, systematic argument drawing carefully on well-selected evidence on teaching and learning which is brought together with personal and professional educational experience and/or their own research to illuminate an integrated discussion.
Independence and initiative	Demonstrates self-direction, independence, originality/ creativity and innovation in tackling and solving problems. Clearly able to select and apply educational ideas to practice in both the candidate's immediate and wider professional contexts.
Evaluation of practice	Evidence of sustained critical evaluation of practices, good awareness of values, assumptions and/or concepts underpinning or influencing pedagogical approaches.
Critical reflection	Provides a critically reflective account demonstrating the ability to synthesise research findings on teaching and learning and to apply them successfully to complex and unpredictable settings.
Presentation	Ideas are communicated in an accomplished and fluent manner consistent with the conventions of writing and presentation for the profession and/or academic discipline, and include a variety of formats where applicable. Compliance with length requirements. Published material is carefully referenced and acknowledged.

Table 4.1   Assessment criteria for work on a PGCE at Master's level

carefully, but don't rely on that alone. It won't pick up every error that you make. Another common crime is unsubstantiated assertion – 'It is well known that…' or 'Girls learn to read more easily than boys.' Who says? Make sure that any texts you've referred to are organised alphabetically in the References section.

Once you're fairly happy with your work, hand it in – or at least leave it alone. Avoid the temptation to hone it to perfection. Accept what is good enough – will it pass? Fine, that's all you need. Now spend your time getting ready for the next deadline.

When you get your work back, don't just look at the grade. Read through all the comments carefully and learn from them so that you get better and better. If they don't mind, read other people's work – particularly ones deemed to be very good so that you know what standard to aspire to.

Lesson planning

Planning lessons is a real skill and one that you'll need to develop. When you're training, it can seem like the hardest thing in the world, but this is what you need to be able to do in order to become a teacher.

> Q22   Plan for progression across the age and ability range for which they are trained, designing effective learning sequences within lessons and across series of lessons and demonstrating secure subject/curriculum knowledge.
>
> Q23   Design opportunities for learners to develop their literacy, numeracy and ICT skills.
>
> (Training and Development Agency for Schools, 2008a)

The different levels of planning – long, medium and short term – can cause confusion.

Long-term plans: these are the areas to teach over the course of each year, based on the NC programmes of study. Your school may well have adapted these, especially if classes are of mixed ages. This long-term plan is broken down into termly or half-termly chunks – the medium-term plans.

Medium-term plans: these are the units of work or main topics that pupils will be taught over a half-term or term. Usually they contain:

- the number of hours or lessons needed;
- the objectives to be covered, adjusted as appropriate for higher and lower attainers;
- opportunities to revisit topics and to make connections between different aspects;
- suggestions for activities;
- time for regular assessment and review.

Short-term plans: these are the plans for one week or lesson. They show the nitty gritty of how a unit of work will unfold to meet the intended objectives.

Long- and medium-term plans should be in place in the schools you go to, so all you have to worry about are translating them into lesson plans. There are lots of published schemes and websites that provide these and that can give you some good ideas. On the standards website (http://nationalstrategies.standards.dcsf.gov.uk), and in published folders that you'll see at college or school, there are very detailed plans. The search facility will help you to find thousands of lesson plans and resources across a wide range of subject areas and age groups. More are added all the time. However, other people's plans won't always work for your particular class and teaching style. You should be creative and confident in adapting or rejecting them to suit your needs.

Activity

Watch Teachers TV programme *The Primary A–Z ... of Lesson Planning* (www.teachers.tv/video/30790).

Seven teachers discuss their tried and tested methods for planning lessons, including breaking lessons into sections, different strategies for engaging children in their lessons, and how to plan for different endings to lessons. They also look how to plan for progression, what can go wrong with planning, and when to step away from your plans and improvise.

Finding the right format for writing the plan is a process that you'll need to go through. Length and detail varies. Some schools require all staff, including trainees, to use a common format such as the one shown in Figure 4.1.

Some people like to script their lessons, others just write down key points. Both are fine – if the lesson is successful. The most useful formats are easy to follow – and you need to be able to read them quickly in case there is a distraction or you lose your train of thought. Most plans have these key elements:

- date, time, subject, class
- learning objective
- assessment criteria
- resources
- teaching points and key questions
- distribution of whole-class and group activities
- what additional adults should do.

Subject:		Class:	Teacher:		Date:		Pd:	NOR:

Prior learning/lesson:

Learning objectives: **Learning outcomes:**

Knowledge:

Understanding:

Skills:

Attitudes and attributes:

Key opportunities for:

Literacy	Numeracy
Extended writing and reading for pleasure	Problem solving
Language	ICT
Model target language	Audience and purpose

Significant contribution to ECM
Enjoy and achieve/Stay safe/Be healthy/Positive contribution/Economic wellbeing

Priority students

SEN inc SA+ boys:	EBD:
EAL:	GAT:

	CMCD*	Activities	Assistant	Assess
Starter Intro	ON TIME CTRT. DOOR MGR REG. MGR - Lates GO-AROUND CUP EQUP/BK MGR	Stand at the door and welcome students. Check uniform. Students enter the room in a quiet and orderly fashion. Reports to be handed to the teacher Learning objectives and/or assessment focus explained. Review last lesson's learning. Hands up to answer.		
Home work	HWK MGR			
Development	INSTRUCTOR TIME SIGN CDTRT** – praise 5 INCH VOICE			
Plenary	EXIT TICKETS	Students stand behind their chairs and are dismissed in small groups. Students leave in an orderly fashion. Bid farewell to the students from your door and greet the next group upon their arrival.		

How do you rate the quality of learning in this lesson? Why?
1. Outstanding   2. Good   3. Satisfactory   4. Inadequate

*CMCD = Consistency Management and Cooperative Discipline
**CDTRT = Caught Doing The Right Thing

Figure 4.1   A lesson plan (Lilian Baylis School, 2009)

Start with the learning objective, chosen from the school's curriculum, then translate it into what you want the pupils to know and understand. First you need to consider what the pupils already know. This is called 'using assessment to inform planning' – one of the standards for qualified teacher status. Good teaching involves the plan–do–assess–plan–do–assess cycle.

If you're not very focused on a specific learning outcome, you'll run into problems. It's tempting to think of activities before considering exactly what the pupils will be learning. For instance, a teacher wrote learning objectives such as 'characteristic features of a period', when 'learning how rich and poor children lived in Victorian times' would have been more precise. If you phrase outcomes as you would tell them to the class, you won't go far wrong. Some people like the acronym WALT – 'we are learning to'. Using such a phrase should help to keep you and the pupils focused. Then you need to think of how to enable pupils to meet objectives, what resources to use, what activities to do and how you'll teach.

If you're new to lesson planning, it's helpful to imagine the lesson and write a chronological plan. Timings – with the resources to be used – can help pace no end. Make your introduction really tight – you can even script the main points. Start by recapping previous learning, sharing the lesson objective (what they'll learn or get better at) and the 'big picture' of the lesson (what's going to happen and in what order).

Plan interesting ways for pupils to learn, but check your ideas with others. I've seen some crazy things. One Year 3 teacher used a *Mr Men* book as the text to teach the literacy strategy objective: 'to discuss characters' feelings, behaviour and relationships, referring to the text'. This was not the level of text that was suitable! Think about different learning styles. People learn through visual, auditory and kinaesthetic (physical interaction) stimuli. Some pupils learn better through one more than another, so aim for a mixture of them.

Differentiation is hard. You need to find out what the highest and lowest attainers can and cannot do, and then plan to allow all to make progress. Different needs can be met in a range of ways, such as:

- the same task that all pupils do with varying degrees of success;
- the same task but with different expectations for different pupils;

- the same task but with different time allocations;
- the same task with an extension activity for the more able;
- adult support to enable low attainers to succeed;
- different resources to help or make the task harder;
- different tasks but the same objective;
- different objectives entirely.

The acronym WILF – 'what I'm looking for' – can help you have realistic but challenging expectations for different pupils. These can also be your assessment criteria. The plenary is an excellent opportunity for you and the pupils to see how the objective of the lesson has been met.

Remember: the better you plan, the better the lesson will go.

Marking

You may have been warned, but nothing really prepares you for the length of time marking takes. Do the rewards, in terms of feedback to pupils that they read and act upon to improve their learning, merit the time spent on marking? I suspect you want to maximise the usefulness of marking, while allowing you time to plan, make and gather resources – and have a life. How long are you spending on marking? Try to keep a record so that you know the scale of the problem. Are you letting marking spread over a longer time than it should? It's so easy to do. If you want to cut down time spent on marking you need to look at whether you're making the most of all the different sorts of marking. Estimate how much marking (of class and homework) you have to do in a week and at what level. Remember that peer review and self-assessment are very valuable, as well as potentially less time consuming for you since you'll be in the role of 'moderator'. Balance out work that needs marking over the week so that you don't have too much to do in one sitting. Decide what seems a realistic amount of time to spend on marking and when you could get it done to fit in with other commitments. Try to stick to your 'timetable', aiming to reduce the time and to do things earlier and more quickly, if possible.

Perhaps you could benefit from extending your range, by considering different sorts of marking:

- children 'marking' their own and each other's work;
- quick-ticking and checking as pupils work;
- using stampers ('good effort', 'excellent!');
- use codes (sp, underline) that pupils understand rather than full sentences;
- selective marking – ignoring all but answers to key questions;
- a brief comment against the learning outcome;
- a detailed comment against the success criteria;
- traffic-light marking – pupils put a green/orange/red mark against work where they feel they've met/partially met/not met the learning outcome.

You'll probably find that different pieces of work require different levels of marking. There will be occasions when a Rolls Royce product is needed, but at other times something more everyday is fine. Once you get to know the expectations of the school and the pupils' work rate, you can design a marking schedule to help you manage what can be a very stressful burden. Ask your colleagues how they manage their marking. How long does it take them? When do they do it? What tips do they have for you? Little things such as collecting books so that they're open at the right page for marking can make a real difference.

Ask to see some examples of other people's marking to get a feel for what is really expected, but avoid the temptation to do a more rigorous job – one-upmanship will generally make your induction year even harder. Do you deliberately plan work that doesn't take so long to mark, but which still meets learning objectives? If you're clear about the learning intention for the lesson, you should be able to write some specific assessment criteria – the things that pupils might do towards meeting the learning intention partially or fully. If you are using worksheets, consider writing assessment criteria directly onto them for you to make some abbreviated judgements against. These can be differentiated for different groups of pupils. For instance, in a lesson on fractions with a mixed-ability class, a teacher wrote success criteria onto the worksheets that they and she could quickly tick, cross or comment on.

Peer review is a very useful form of marking. Plan some time for pupils to swap books and 'mark' each other's. Ideally do this before the end of the lesson so they can improve their work before the lesson finishes. This will be truly formative marking. Pupils are rarely silly or rude about each other's work, but you'll need to consider your pairings carefully and come down hard on those who do not approach their responsibilities sensibly. Putting people who are friends and whose work is of a similar standard together works well. If you have an assistant, deploy them to help those who have difficulty reading and writing. Pairing people who speak the same mother tongue can also be advantageous, because they can explain things to each other in their own language.

Pupils will copy the marking style they have experienced, so your one-to-one marking will have countless spin-offs. The above procedure will also be useful for you to use. Follow the school or department marking policy and decide on your own additional one. Note points that many pupils had difficulty with on a lesson plan, so that it can feed into teaching. Try to focus on marking against assessment criteria – how well they have met the learning objectives. This is easier said than done, particularly in a piece full of errors. What are you going to do about spelling mistakes, for instance? What about handwriting, grammar and punctuation? When will the pupils have time to read and respond to your marking, by correcting and learning spellings for example?

Managing behaviour

Managing behaviour is one of the greatest concerns of new teachers. This book can't hope to give much help on such a complex and important topic, but there is no shortage of ones devoted to the topic. Half of the battle for control lies in being organised, planning the right sort of work and being confident. Many people who have turned out to be very good teachers started with very demanding discipline problems – so take heart, things do get better.

If you are having difficulty with control, you need extra support – urgently – in establishing and maintaining the school's, and your own, behaviour policy. At a practical level, it's useful to have someone who will take miscreants off you, and someone to read the riot act for or with you. The chance word of a friend, 'Nil illegitimi carborundum', 'Don't let the b******s get you down', when I was having problems with a class as an experienced teacher, gave me the resolve not to give up. I changed tack, turning from a sensitive, fair teacher to a hard, dictator-like person who was not going to let the class beat her and who ruled with a rod of iron. It worked.

Getting and keeping attention are common problems. The secret is to keep lots of strategies up your sleeve. After a while, even the best ones get stale and you need to do something new. Whatever you do, try to minimise your voice being used and time being wasted. Here are some ideas from a range of beginning teachers.

1. The more negative I am and the more I shout, the more the pupils make noise. Be calm and positive: this gives the impression that you are in control.

2. Laminate each pupil's name onto card and affix it to a board with blu-tack or Velcro. Stick a smiley face at the top of the board and agree rewards for the pupils whose names are still on the board at the end of the day/week. Clearly establish the kinds of behaviour which will result in names staying on the board.

3. Football card system. Cut up squares of red and yellow card. Like a football referee, a pupil who misbehaves is given a warning, and then a yellow card. This means that if the pupil misbehaves again, he or she will get a red card. They spend a set length of time writing about exactly what they have done wrong to get the cards and what they will do in the future. You then file this 'signed confession' as it can be used as evidence later.

4. Let them have noisy moments. I've learned to anticipate that they will have noisy moments between lessons, etc., and things have become easier since I stopped expecting them to be quiet all the time.

5. I just stop and stare at them with a 'you know you are in the wrong, now do what I want' look and they shut up!

6. Simply stand at the front and raise one arm. As each pupil notices he/she raises an arm and stops talking. No one wants to be the last so they all quickly quieten down and listen.

7. Fire out the rewards (stickers, etc.). If you spot a couple of quiet pupils, then reward them! The rest will soon follow suit.

8. Every Friday they have 30 minutes 'golden time' where they can choose what to do. Taking off minutes of this time (or even threatening to) for bad behaviour works a treat.
9. Get them into the routine of coming in and doing something: handwriting, number bonds, times tables, maths challenges, anything really, the more fun (and absorbing) the better!
10. To get everyone's attention call '3, 2, 1 silence'; bang a drum, cymbal, etc.; clap a rhythm for them to copy or 'answer'; turn the lights off.

Graduated responses

You need to think creatively about solutions to the numerous, everyday irritating behaviours, such as:

- calling out
- fiddling
- tapping
- talking when you're talking
- the whine – 'Miiiiiiisss'
- hair-dressing
- being out of their seats
- farting – and the fuss from other pupils.

Just take one or two of the things that wind you up and think how you usually handle it, and then all the alternative ways you could do so. Think of your potential responses, ranging from cool to very hot, slow to breaking the speed limit. Have a look at Figure 4.2 to see graduated responses to positive and negative behaviour. You need to give yourself plenty of room for manoeuvre, so go for calm strategies at first rather than going for the jugular straight away. You need to stay polite, calm and cool and leave room for manoeuvre. Losing your temper does your blood pressure no good and normally makes you look ridiculous as you splutter and rant.

Remember that you, as a teacher, are a manager of incidents as well as of teaching materials, furniture, curriculum, etc. What you do or say can vary the incident in just as significant a way as the person causing the disruption. Teachers can unwittingly escalate

Positive behaviour		Negative behaviour
Eye contact	1	Eye contact
Smile	2	Move close to
Thumbs up	3	Cross look
'Well done' personal	4	Rule reminder
'Well done' publicly in class	5	Praise nearby people who are doing the right thing
Star	6	Give choices
Team point	7	Warning 1: name on board
Special responsibility	8	Warning 2: lose minutes off break
Recognition by another member of staff	9	Warning 3: lose all break
Recognition by headteacher	10	Send to another member of staff
Whole-school recognition	11	Send to headteacher
Recognition sent to parents, e.g. letter	12	Inform parents

Figure 4.2 Graduated responses to positive and negative behaviour

problems by failing to consider alternative strategies or predicting likely responses. Most disruptive incidents can be anticipated and predicted. Teachers need to prepare for discipline as rigorously as any aspect of the curriculum.

Learning from observing others

Whatever stage you're at in the profession, you'll learn a great deal about teaching from watching others doing it. Similarly, the more you watch children learning, and think about the problems that they have, the better your teaching will be. Make the most of your training opportunities to observe other teachers. Try to watch a range of teachers and assistants, age groups, subjects and lessons at different times of the day. It's very cheering to see that everyone has similar problems and fascinating to study the different ways people manage them. Don't always observe experienced and successful teachers. You'll learn a great deal from seeing other trainees, new teachers, assistants and supply teachers. If you watch a class you've taught being led by someone else, you can see the pupils' learning, behaviour and reactions, and how another teacher handles them.

However, observing so that you get something out of it is not easy. You need to have a focus for your observation. There is so much to see that you can end up getting overwhelmed. First, decide what you want to observe. Ideally, link the observation to something that you have problems with or want to develop. For instance, if you want to improve pace in introductions, arrange to observe that. Notice the speed of the exposition, how many pupils answer questions and how the teacher manages to move them on, how instructions are given and resources distributed, and how off-task behaviour is dealt with.

Once you have decided what you'd like to observe, you need to arrange it. You need to discuss what you want to observe with the teacher. Remember that they're doing you a favour and may be apprehensive about you being in the classroom so you'll need to be sensitive. Tell them what you'd like to see and why. Ask if you can look at planning related to the lesson. It's essential to look at teaching in relation to learning. Always think about cause and effect. Why are the pupils behaving as they are? The cause is usually related to teaching.

Make sure you sit where you can see both the teacher and the pupils, and look at what high, average and low attainers accomplish. Jot down things of interest. You may want to note certain phrases the teacher uses to get attention, the way they organise tidying-up time, etc. You can use a blank piece of paper for this, but a form with prompts (Figure 4.3) helps to keep you focused.

Teacher: Subject: Learning objective:	Date and time: Additional adults:
Prompts	Comments. What has the teacher done to get this response?
Behave well *Relate well to adults and pupils* *Understand what to do* *Understand what they're learning* *Gain new knowledge, skills* *Speak and listen well* *Work hard* *Act responsibly* *Understand how well they have done* *Understand how they can improve* *Enjoy the lesson*	

Figure 4.3 Lesson observation: how well pupils learn

The Insider's Guide for New Teachers, Routledge © Sara Bubb 2010

Afterwards, reflect on the teaching and learning you've seen – ideally in discussion with the person you observed. Perhaps it inspired a brainwave, unrelated to what you saw. Write a few bullet points about what you've learned, and the ideas that could be implemented.

Being observed

You'll probably be observed about once per week when you're training. It's almost always a stressful experience, but try to see it as an opportunity to get some really useful feedback and as a way to develop – not as a threat. The value of observation, however, depends on how well it is planned, executed and discussed afterwards.

The people observing you may also find it stressful. Much teacher training is done in partnership with schools, so you may have people observing you who feel inexperienced and uncertain of the best way to go about it. They will also be mindful of the responsibility to help you make progress, while maintaining a good relationship. This can lead some to be too kind. Trainees sometimes feel that they are not being sufficiently challenged. This is particularly true if you're very successful, but you too need to be helped to develop professionally. You can help this process by being very open to ideas and accepting and even encouraging constructive criticism. Phrases, such as 'That's a really good idea, thanks', will work wonders.

Before an observation

To get the most from an observation, think about what you'd like the observer to look out for: a problem you're having. Far from being an admission of failure, this will show that you're a reflective practitioner who wants to improve. You'll feel better about the observation if you're completely prepared. If you know when you'll be seen, plan with even more care and have a copy of the lesson plan for the observer. Be absolutely clear about what you want the pupils to learn and achieve by the end of the lesson, and make sure that your teaching and the activities enable them to do so. Really think through every stage of the lesson to pre-empt problems – transitions from one thing to another are usually tricky. Have as much as possible written on the board beforehand.

Think about what the person observing you is looking for. Address things that haven't gone well before. Look at the standards again. Obviously, you'll want to show that you're making progress against your current objectives too. Look at the form that the observation will be written on. All observers have their own pet loves and hates that will affect how they look at your teaching, so plan to please!

Most importantly, look after yourself so that you're on top form for the lesson that will be observed. Try to get a good night's sleep the night before so you're not too tired. Eat and drink things that make you feel good. Avoid too much caffeine. Do everything you can to feel confident – wear your favourite teaching clothes, encourage other people to boost you up. Tell yourself that you're going to teach well, and believe it.

Coping with nerves

Being nervous when observed is perfectly normal, and most people can tell when you are and make allowances for this. One way of coping with nerves is to understand why you get worried: then you can do something about it. Here are some common concerns and possible solutions.

Pupils will be passive, won't engage, answer questions, etc.

- Plan something to get them lively; use talk partners ('turn to your neighbour and tell them the answer to my question').

The behaviour of a certain child will ruin everything.

- Ask someone else to have the child for that lesson; plan for an assistant to be with the child; warn the observer.

I can't get or keep attention.

- Do your best; plan well with this in mind; keep the pace going; try suggested strategies; have as much written on the board beforehand as possible; warn the observer; look on the observation as a way to get really specific advice.

The pupils play up when I'm observed.

- Tell them that they are being observed. Remind them that you are expecting exemplary behaviour.

Technology will go wrong.

- Set it up beforehand; check and double check; have a back up if it does go wrong.

I'll forget or lose key resources.

- Make a list of what you need, tick items off when collected, organise them.

The teaching assistant won't turn up.

- Keep reminding them that you're relying on them and give them a plan of what they should do.

Some pupils will finish work too early.

- Have some extension work; make the task harder or open-ended.

I'll forget what I planned to do.

- Do a clear written plan (that very act helps lodge it in your mind); keep your plan to hand on a distinctive clipboard to avoid it getting lost; have a spare just in case you leave it somewhere; use prompt cards; rehearse the lesson structure in your mind.

I'll forget what to say.

- Script key parts of the lesson, especially questions; rehearse out-loud and in your head; have as much as possible on the board.

I'll let the class wander off the point of the lesson.

- Stay focused; put timings on your plan; display the learning objective; plan questions that will guide the pupils' thinking.

During the observation

Give the observer a copy of your plan so that they are clear why you are doing certain things, but otherwise just block out the observer and focus on teaching and learning. Think of your teaching as a performance, and go for gold. Try to keep to time, but be flexible where necessary. Pupils' learning is more important than sticking to your plan. Don't forget to have a plenary to reinforce and assess learning. Try to demonstrate the standards. Be particularly organised with resources. Don't feel inhibited by the presence of the observer – try to be natural.

Don't panic if things start to go wrong. Think on your feet. Most trainees have some lessons that go swimmingly, others that are okay and some that are a disaster. There are a huge number of factors to do with you and what you're teaching, and then a whole heap more to do with different classes, what lesson they've just had, what the weather is like and what time of day it is.

The post-observation discussion

After the lesson, think about what the pupils learned and why, so that you're ready to answer the inevitable 'How do you think it went?' question. What were you pleased with? What could have gone better? How did your teaching affect the progress pupils made? Don't be disheartened if the lesson didn't go well. See it as an event to be learnt from and given advice on. It was a one-off performance, a snap-shot, and things can be different tomorrow.

Use the feedback to discuss the minutiae of the lesson, and to get ideas for improvements. There is no such thing as a perfect teacher (except in your mind), so your lesson doesn't have to be perfect. You need to show that you're reflective, making progress and acting on advice. Most of all, show that you want advice – don't be defensive. Be aware of your body language and notice that of the person giving you feedback. You want to come across as earnest and reflective. A large proportion of communication is non-verbal, so:

- lean slightly forward;
- uncross your arms;
- make eye contact;
- smile and nod;
- listen actively.

Listen well: don't just hear what you want or expect to hear. Focus on what is being said rather than how it is being said, and see it as information rather than criticism. Make notes of salient points. Paraphrase and summarise what the observer says. This helps you concentrate on what is being said and is very helpful in getting a clear understanding of their view. It involves reflecting back your interpretation of what you have heard, which can be very useful for the observer. Use phrases such as 'So what you mean is…' and 'In other words…'.

However, if you think your teaching is criticised unfairly, make sure you explain the reasoning behind your actions. Stick up for yourself, though in an utterly professional way. Ask for clarification of anything you're unsure of, and examples and suggestions of how you could have done things differently. Try to get lots of advice and ideas that you can go away with and mull over. Afterwards, reflect on the discussion. Feel good about the positive comments (there will always be some) and think about how to improve. Set yourself targets of things to do better.

Teaching is a physically, mentally and emotionally demanding job. You need to look after yourself if you are going to succeed. This is the focus of the next chapter.

five

Looking after yourself

- Stages you might go through
- Looking after yourself
- Looking after your voice
- Managing your time

Your training and the first year in teaching will be rewarding and stimulating, but it will undoubtedly be hard and very stressful. In this chapter I will look at ways to make it easier on a very practical level.

Stages you might go through

There is a common perception that a teacher should be able to teach well. Certainly, the pupils taught by a trainee or NQT have as much right to a good education as those taught by someone with 20 years of experience. However, there is a huge difference between novice and experienced teachers. Like any skill or craft, learning to teach is a developmental process characterised by devastating disasters and spectacular successes. Teaching is a job that can never be done perfectly – one can always improve. The more I know about teaching and learning the more I realise there is to know. This is what makes it such a great job – but also such a potentially depressing one.

How you feel about teaching will probably change on a daily basis at first. One day will be great and leave you feeling positive and idealistic, but the next will be diabolical. As time goes on, good days outnumber the bad ones, and you will realise that you are actually enjoying the job. There are recognised stages that

Stage	Characteristics
Early idealism	Feeling that everything is possible and having a strong picture of how you want to teach ('I'll never shout'). This is a fantasy stage where you imagine pupils hanging on your every word.
Survival	Reality strikes. You live from day to day, needing quick fixes and tips. You find it hard to solve problems because there are so many of them. Behaviour management is of particular concern – you have nightmares about losing control. You are too stressed and busy to reflect. Colds and sore throats seem permanent. Survival often characterises the middle of teaching practice and the second half of the first term for NQTs.
Recognising difficulties	You can see problems more clearly. You can identify difficulties and think of solutions because there is some space in your life. You move forward. A skilled mentor or induction tutor aids this stage considerably.
Hitting the plateau	Key problems, such as behaviour management and organisation, have been solved so you feel things are going well. You feel you are mastering teaching. You begin to enjoy it and don't find it too hard, but you don't want to tackle anything different or take on any radical new initiatives. If forced, you will pay lip service to new developments. Some teachers spend the rest of their career at this stage.
Moving on	You are ready for further challenges. You want to try out different styles of teaching, new age groups, take on more responsibilities.

Activity
What stage do you think you are in at the moment?
Where do you want to be and by when?
What can you do to move on?
Who can help you?

Figure 5.1   Five stages that teachers go through (source: based on Maynard and Furlong 1995)

teachers go through. Recognising them will help to keep you going and help you realise that you will need different levels and types of support at different times during your training and induction years. I have used Furlong and Maynard's (1995) five stages of development that teachers go through to illustrate the development that might happen to you (see Figure 5.1).

Looking after yourself

If your experiences are like mine, illness will plague you during your training and first year of teaching like it has never done before. By 'illness', I am not talking about anything serious – just the low-level depressing rounds of sore throats, coughs and colds. Large numbers of children means a lot of germs! When you're busy, the easiest thing to do is to forget to look after yourself. Everyone knows that they function better with good nutrition and rest, but these seem to be the first things to be neglected.

Are you getting irritable, tired, anxious, depressed, forgetful or accident-prone? Do you have aches and pains, headaches, digestive problems or seem to succumb to every germ that's doing the rounds? They are signals to you from your body that should not be ignored for long. Teaching is a stressful job and when you're new it's even worse, so it's nothing to be ashamed about. Stress is defined as 'the adverse reaction people have to excessive pressures or other types of demand placed upon them. It arises when they worry they can't cope.' Stress affects different people in different ways, but you need to cope with the results of it and handle the causes. Given that there is no single cause of stress, there's no simple solution.

Stress management is a process, not a simple repair job. Look out for behaviour, mental health and physical symptoms. The first step is to recognise that the problem exists and tell someone how you feel – almost all teachers are kind and caring, but they can't help you unless they know what the problem is. The Teacher Support Network (TSN) (www.teachersupport.info) has an excellent online stress assessment you can use to identify your levels of stress. It gives you a report which you can email to anyone else that you think might benefit from knowing the result. It also contains suggestions for coping better. The Teacher Support Line is open every day and staffed by trained counsellors.

Analyse the causes of your stress. You need to be very honest with yourself. Try listing all your troubles, then dividing them into those over which you have some control, and those which you haven't. Work on practical solutions to those over which you have some influence.

Teaching makes you feel very tired, but exercise will give you more energy. You function better all around if you are fit. This could mean taking up jogging or going to the local gym, but even a quick 20-minute walk can help and that's something you can start on today.

Relax. Recovering from the 'high alert' positions that our bodies may have been in for long periods during the day is important, but hard to do. Do something that forces you to think about something other than work, something that needs your active involvement. A good quality and quantity of sleep is a must too. You need to be in tip-top form to teach, so invest in your body!

Remember to eat – don't skip meals. Watch your caffeine and biscuit intake – the staple diet of many staff rooms! They really aren't much good for you. Snack on nutritious, high-energy foods such as bananas rather than chocolate bars. Get organised at week-ends so that you have enough suitable food to last the week. Consider vitamin supplements. Vitamins and minerals are essential in helping your body fight off all the viruses that the pupils will bring into school. Some people swear by *Echinacea*.

Plan some 'me' time into your life. Do whatever makes you feel better. This might be soaking in a hot bath, reading novels or watching escapist films. Also, keep a social life. This is likely to be limited, but is essential.

See teaching as acting. Each lesson is a performance, and if one goes badly the next can go better. Separate the performance from the real you. This will stop you feeling too wretched about lessons that don't go well. Remember that few people are natural-born teachers – everyone has to work at it and everyone can get better.

Looking after your voice

Perhaps one of the most important tools teachers have is their voice – without it we are lost. Teachers use their voices as much as the busiest professional actor, but do so day-in and day-out, and without training. Tension restricts your voice and can cause lasting damage. In training and your first year of teaching, if not throughout your career, you are likely to suffer problems with your voice. It is worth trying to look after it. Here are some examples of things that are bad for your voice:

- excessive or forceful coughing or throat clearing – these put a great strain on your voice and are often habits rather than physical necessities;

- drinking tea, coffee, fizzy drinks or alcohol – these dehydrate the body;
- constantly placing demands on the voice, such as shouting or speaking above pupils;
- speaking or singing when the voice is tired or sore;
- whispering – this is just as harmful as shouting because it strains the voice;
- speaking in a forceful or tense manner;
- being tense – the voice is part of the muscle and breathing system, both of which suffer when you are stressed, so the ability to relax is essential;
- smoke, chalk dust, felt-tip pen fumes, chlorine, etc. are all bad for your voice;
- continuing to use a sore throat, using maskers such as pain-killers, throat sweets or sprays that provide temporary relief.

Ideas for looking after your voice

Think of all the strategies you can use to engage your pupils that don't involve your voice. Consider: body language, signals and gesture; where you position yourself; encouraging and developing pupils' listening skills; agreed signals (whistle, song, time-out gesture) and how you can draw their attention to you. Find non-verbal ways to get attention. You might use a drum, cymbal or triangle, clap a rhythm that the pupils have to repeat back to you, or raise a hand. Develop more non-verbal communication. The look, the smile, the glare, the raised eyebrow, the 'tut' can be more effective than words – and so can a theatrical silence or closing of a book. Listen to yourself teaching (use a tape recorder) – are you using enough intonation to keep attention, unnecessarily repeating things, talking over the pupils or talking too much? Other tips include:

- Drink more water. Aim for six to eight glasses of still water each day.
- For more volume without shouting, project your voice. Open your mouth more and try to speak from the lungs rather than the throat.
- Inhale steam if you have a tired or sore throat.

- Breathe in a relaxed, focused manner, avoiding lifting shoulders and upper chest.
- Find someone to massage your neck and shoulders to relax this area.
- Allow your voice periods of rest.
- In the classroom, use your voice with care and economy. Aim to say things only once – some teachers get into the habit of repeating almost everything they say!
- When whole-class teaching, emphasise key words orally, and write them on the board for added effect.
- Where possible, move to your listeners rather than calling out. Position yourself so that everyone can see your lips and hear you at your most comfortable volume.
- Plan for learning to occur through pupil-talk rather than always through teacher-talk.
- If you need to shout, only shout the first word, then quieten down. For instance, 'STOP what you're doing and look this way.' Lower the pitch to sound more authoritative and avoid squeaking.
- Don't try to talk over pupils. If you talk while they are chatting they might stop talking, but the chances are they'll just carry on at a greater volume.
- Don't cough to clear your throat too often – swallow or yawn instead.

Look out for damage to your voice, for which you should seek medical advice:

- a hoarse voice that persists;
- change in vocal quality, pitch, sudden shifts in pitch, breaks in the voice;
- vocal fatigue for no apparent reason;
- tremors in the voice;
- pain while speaking;
- loss of voice.

Managing your time

If you're to survive, let alone make the most of your training years, you need to get into the habit of using your time well. Perhaps you're already ruthlessly efficient in this area; one of those people for whom even trash-TV watching seems to be purposeful. Most people, however, feel that they have too much to do in too little time. It's one of the main reasons people give for leaving the profession. It's such a problem that a great deal of time and money have been spent on restructuring the teaching workforce so that everyone can (in theory) work fewer hours, and spend time on the most useful aspects of the job. Get into good habits while you're training.

Knowing how you're spending time

Whether you're at college or in a school, it's useful to see how you spend your time. Complete Figure 5.2 for one week to get a feel for whether you have a work–life balance. 'Me time' should include anything that you feel better for, such as socialising, going out, exercising, watching a favourite TV programme, reading, soaking in the bath or talking to someone you like. Under

	Working at school/college	Working at home	Travel for work	Domestic	Me time	Sleep
Sun						
Mon						
Tues						
Weds						
Thurs						
Fri						
Sat						
Total						

Figure 5.2 How do you spend your time?

The Insider's Guide for New Teachers, Routledge © Sara Bubb 2010

'domestic' put basic everyday living – cooking, shopping, tidying, washing, cleaning, talking to people at home and eating.

You don't have to be precise in allocating time, but does each day add up roughly to 24 hours? If it's under, maybe you, like me, find that time just disappears. This is lovely if you're on holiday – in fact it's one of the marks of a relaxed day when I can't think what I've done with my time … and I don't care. When you're becoming a teacher though, disappearing hours can be dangerous because there's just too much to do and you'll get behind.

Look at your chart. What are you doing too little of? If you don't get enough sleep, noisy classrooms are unbearable so that's a definite one to keep an eye on. Is there anyway that travel time can be reduced by, say, going to work or college before the morning rush hour and leaving before the evening one? If you use public transport, could you get anything done during travel time – marking, planning, thinking, some 'me time' reading, or a quick nap? A journey can be a good way to wind down after a day's work. I know a teacher who returned to her old job that had a long journey because the new one had a journey so short that there seemed to be no gap between work and home, so no winding down. For those of you with dependents at home, travelling may be the only time you get to yourself.

Using time well

It's useful to think about the quality of your time, as well as the quantity available. It's worth recognising which part of the day – or night – is the most productive for you, the time when you have your most creative ideas or can concentrate best. For the majority of people, this time is early in the day, when they are at their most fresh. A minority of people do their best work late at night.

About 20 per cent of our time is prime time and, used well, it should produce about 80 per cent of our most creative and productive work. The rest of your time is likely to be of lower quality, and is nowhere near as productive. In this low-quality time, plan to do things that are easy to pick up after interruptions, or jobs that we look forward to doing. Lesson planning, writing essays and other difficult jobs need high-quality time. If you try to do them at times when you'll be interrupted, tired and hungry you'll become frustrated, and everything will take longer. You also need to consider where you work best.

It seems to be the done thing, in some schools and colleges at least, to stay as long as possible – presentism – and there's definitely a competitive element to it. I've known people who came in at 7.00 a.m. or 7.30 a.m. and stayed until 5.30 p.m. or later, and still went home with huge amounts of work. Let's face it, if you are a teacher who cares even a little bit about the quality of work you do, you will be investing massive amounts of your own time on the job outside of directed hours. Indeed, you could work all the time if you were so inclined and still have more things to do. Evenings, weekends, holidays. There's always room for work. Pace yourself. Plan some days to be less demanding. Recognise the peaks and troughs in your daily energy levels and organise yourself accordingly. Set yourself time limits and work limits – and stick to them.

The education system is committed to reducing teacher workload through what's called the Remodelling Agreement. The following tasks should not routinely be carried out by teachers, but by support staff:

1. collecting money;
2. chasing absences: teachers will need to inform the relevant member of staff when students are absent from their class or from school;
3. bulk photocopying;
4. copy typing;
5. producing standard letters: teachers may be required to contribute as appropriate in formulating the content of standard letters;
6. producing class lists: teachers may be required to be involved as appropriate in allocating students to a particular class;
7. record keeping and filing: teachers may be required to contribute to the content of records;
8. classroom display: teachers will make professional decisions in determining what material is displayed in and around their classroom;
9. analysing attendance figures: it is for teachers to make use of the outcome of analysis;

10. processing exam results: teachers will need to use the analysis of exam results;
11. collating pupil reports;
12. administering work experience: teachers may be required to support pupils on work experience (including through advice and visits);
13. administering examinations: teachers have a professional responsibility for identifying appropriate examinations for their pupils;
14. administering teacher cover;
15. ICT troubleshooting and minor repairs;
16. commissioning new ICT equipment;
17. ordering supplies and equipment: teachers may be involved in identifying needs;
18. stocktaking;
19. cataloguing, preparing, issuing and maintaining equipment and materials;
20. minuting meetings: teachers may be required to communicate action points from meetings;
21. coordinating and submitting bids: teachers may be required to make a professional input into the content of bids;
22. seeking and giving personnel advice;
23. managing pupil data: teachers will need to make use of the analysis of pupil data;
24. inputting pupil data: teachers will need to make the initial entry of pupil data into school management systems.

(DFES, 2003: p.5)

Work smarter not harder

The trick is to prioritise so that the essential things get done, and that what doesn't get done has minimal consequences. So, what is the most important thing? Don't be a perfectionist – 'good enough' will do because the risk of burn-out is very real. The profession is haemorrhaging people leaving within the first five years. You, as the new generation of teachers, need to make this job manageable so that you stick with it – and enjoy it. Here are some tips – you probably know them already, but do you do them?

- prioritise;
- compartmentalise – set boundaries, especially when working at home;
- accept 'good enough';
- avoid stressful people and time bandits;
- set yourself targets – don't add to them;
- when do you work best? Fit work around energy highs and lows;
- what work can be done in lows?;
- set boundaries to tasks – time, quality, quantity;
- build in rewards;
- draw up an action plan of how you'll reduce time on specific tasks, such as the one in Figure 5.3.

It will be important to look after yourself, not only during your training, but when you are employed as a teacher. But what sort of teaching job are you looking for? The next chapter will help you understand the options.

Date:		
I want to spend less time on .... At the moment I spend ...... minutes a week on it, but I want to reduce it to ...... minutes by		
I am going to do this by...	When	Progress notes

Review notes

Figure 5.3   An action plan to reduce worktime

The Insider's Guide for New Teachers, Routledge © Sara Bubb 2010

Your first year

six

Looking for a job

Which country?

Financial incentives

Types of school

Supply teaching

Moving between primary, secondary and special

What sort of school will suit you?

Where to look for a job

There's a great deal to consider when thinking about working as a teacher. There are so many different schools out there. You need to factor into the equation: financial incentives, whether to opt for the independent or state sector, supply teaching, working abroad, moving between primary, secondary and special, and what sort of school will suit you so that you're clear about what you want.

Which country?

Even before you think about which school, you should decide which country to work in. Most people teach in the country they trained in, but moving even within the UK can be difficult because the regulations and induction systems vary. However, each country within the EEA recognises each other's induction qualifications, so you won't have to repeat your first year if you move.

The entry qualifications to be a teacher differ between England, Scotland, Northern Ireland and Wales. For instance, the General Teaching Council of Scotland (GTCS) is very rigorous about qualifications and you must register in order to teach. The PGCE and BEd are recognised by the GTCS, but the GTP and RTP are not. You have to register for the subject you trained to teach, and the GTCS are strict about you having a degree in that subject. For instance, people registering as English teachers must have a degree with at least 80 credit points in English, of which at least 40 credit points must be in English literature or Scottish literature. Music teachers must have a degree with at least 80 credits in music and which includes studying music over at least three years. The degree must include the following:

- The study of harmony, counterpoint, arrangement, orchestration and composition, together with a broad study of music in its social and historical contexts within traditional, ethnic and non-western musical cultures.
- Keyboard studies including sight reading, playing by ear, accompanying, harmonising and improvising in traditional and contemporary styles.
- Studying an instrument or voice to an advanced standard.

(www.gtcs.gov.uk)

You may want to work further afield, outside Europe. No matter how good the support is for new teachers or how British the school, it won't count as induction for UK purposes, so you'll have to do induction in England when you return. There isn't any time limit between getting your teaching qualification and starting your induction year in England, though lots of people think there is. Your QTS never runs out and can't be taken away from you. You've got it for life. However, you can fail induction, which means you aren't allowed to teach in a state school or non-maintained special school in England ever again. So it makes sense to do induction in your first year of teaching when all that you've learnt is fresh and up-to-date, and in the context that you trained for. Going abroad is going to make a complex job harder, and you won't get the reduced timetable, support, monitoring and assessment that will help you be a better teacher.

Having taught abroad won't be detrimental to getting employment in England – but I don't suppose it'll help if you're competing with people fresh from training and up-to-date with the latest educational developments. Employers may feel that your professionalism has been enriched through teaching abroad or they may question your commitment to the job and to staying at their school. There will always be schools with vacancies, but these are often ones in 'challenging circumstances' with a high staff turnover – not brilliant places to do induction.

You also need to question whether you should teach abroad when your own country has invested in training you and needs you desperately. Working abroad may seem glamorous, especially when you're interviewed in a swanky London hotel, but many people tell a very different story – as the quotes below indicate – so do research the school carefully before signing any contract.

Every time my employers decide to make cutbacks they change our contracts, altering bonuses, etc. Unfortunately we have to accept or leave.

They do not put money into staff training.

Normally what you are told in interviews is often what you want to hear. They talk of palm trees, the Red Sea, amazing pupil–teacher ratios and the tax-free salary. It feels different when you get into the classroom and face 27 very mixed ability, mixed English, indifferent, rude, obnoxious pupils.

English is not widely spoken so you may feel isolated if you come by yourself.

Resources were few, communication was poor, there appeared to be no genuine educational vision and the school did not enforce its own rules and published standards.

They are into making money, and you are going to help them make money!

Despite the glossy brochures and many promises, when I arrived there was a 100 per cent new staff!

Many schools do not appear to have a salary structure they are willing to make public.

Living abroad is a culture shock.

International schools range from the appalling to the outstanding. Before accepting a teaching position, speak to or email someone who works at the school and ask specific questions about salary, accommodation, classroom resources, the sorts of pupils and teaching workload.

Financial incentives

There are four separate scales on the main pay scale (MPS) depending on whether you work in inner, outer or the fringe of London, or elsewhere in England and Wales. There's nearly £4,000 difference between the areas, so it pays to be strategic. Of the capital's 33 boroughs, those that border a county are classed as outer London and all others are inner London. Ealing, Barking & Dagenham, Haringey and Merton are classed as inner London, even though they seem quite far out and have cheaper housing. There are no easy rules about fringe payments, but you get it as far out as places like Thurrock and Hatfield.

England and Wales have financial incentives for teachers of shortage subjects, which you'll want to bear in mind when deciding what sort of school you want to work in.

National Challenge schools

Schools where fewer than 30 per cent of pupils get five GCSEs at A–C, including English and Maths, are part of the National Challenge programme. This provides extra money and help. People who choose to work in one of these 420 schools will get a £10,000 loyalty payment after three years of service. New teachers will also be eligible for a priority place on the MTL, which is an innovative practice-based MA qualification for teachers that will further develop their professional knowledge and skills.

Golden Hellos

If you get a job in a maintained secondary school, you can claim the £5,000 Golden Hello in England and Wales if you did a PGCE in secondary Maths or Science. English, modern foreign languages, Welsh, Design and Technology or Information and

Communications Technology (ICT) secondary PGCEs carry a £2,500 Golden Hello. You claim the money during the year after you've successfully completed induction if you are still teaching that shortage subject in a maintained school for at least half of your timetable. The money is subject to tax and national insurance. You will not be eligible for a Golden Hello in schools that are not state-maintained, such as private schools.

In order to actually claim the Golden Hello you have to fill in the form that you were probably given when you were training, and submit it to your school, who will then send it to the LA for payment. If you've lost it, you can get another from the organisation that you did your PGCE with: the training provider needs to complete the first section which confirms that you undertook an eligible course.

You don't need to have been in continuous employment for the Golden Hello. In fact, you can have about three-and-a-half years out, since the rule is that you can have the Golden Hello as long as within five years of qualifying as a teacher you have finished induction (one-year minimum) and are working in a state school. You just need proof that you've passed induction.

> My PGCE was in Business Studies but I've now finished induction and am teaching Maths in a state school. Am I eligible for the Golden Hello?

> I did a Maths PGCE last year and currently teach at a primary school, so am I eligible for a Golden Hello?

You have to be teaching the shortage subject that you qualified in, so the people above would not be eligible for the Golden Hello.

Types of school

Maintained sector

Most schools are in the maintained sector, which means that they are funded and controlled by the state. However, there are lots of different schools around. Most are maintained by the DCSF and LAs and are known as 'community schools', though ones with

Foundation school status have more independence from the LA. The governing body, rather than the LA, is the employer and the admissions authority. Some schools have awards or specialist status. Others are based around a certain faith. Adverts usually refer to what status or awards the school has. The most common awards are:

- Artsmark, for excellence in the arts – there are different levels, the top of which is gold.
- Sportsmark, for excellence in sport.
- Investors in People – an award for organisations that look after their staff well.
- School achievement award – awarded to schools which have vastly improved their test and exam results.

There is a confusing array of types of schools – and one school can carry several labels and hold several awards. There are specialist schools, training schools, academies and faith schools.

Specialist schools

Specialist schools have been designated by the government to have a special focus on their chosen subject area. They must meet the full NC requirements and deliver a broad and balanced education to all pupils, as well as specialising in their chosen subject area. Specialist schools are expected to work with other schools and the local community, sharing their specialist resources and expertise so that everybody in the community benefits.

Training schools

Training schools are very successful and are funded to facilitate networks of schools and teacher training institutions, and help to develop and implement ITT.

Academies

Academies are publicly funded independent schools, which tend to be state-of-the-art, all-ability specialist schools established by sponsors from business, faith or voluntary groups working with partners from the local community. Sponsors and the Department for Children, Schools and Families (DCSF) provide the capital costs for an academy, with running costs met in full by the DCSF.

Faith schools

Many faith schools are within the state sector, although some are fee-paying. They prefer teachers and pupils of that faith, although they vary in how strict they are about this. Adverts often say something like: 'Applications are welcome from Catholics and other teachers who feel they can make an active contribution to the aims, values and activities of the school.'

Faith schools are either voluntary aided (VA) or voluntary controlled (VC), depending on the level of autonomy they have opted for. The LA is the employer and the admissions authority in VC schools. The governing body is the employer and the admissions authority in VA schools.

Independent schools

The first thing you need to consider is whether you should go into the independent sector. Table 6.1 lists advantages and disadvantages. Many independent schools are very good, but some are appalling. There is still some mistrust and prejudice between the maintained and private sectors, and limited movement between the two, so you need to be aware that you may find it hard to get a job in a state school if you start in an independent. You should certainly check that the independent school teaches the NC in the same way as a state school – and that it keeps up-to-date with national developments. Some independents can be rather traditional and conservative, and you don't want that to hinder your development as a teacher.

Induction is optional in the independent sector, though most offer and encourage it, but you need to complete induction in order to be able to teach in a state school in England in the future. More importantly, induction will help you through your first year and make you a better teacher, so it's important to undergo it as soon as possible – for your and your pupils' sakes. However, the very fact that it is optional causes problems:

Advantages	Disadvantages
Pupils may be better behaved and motivated	Different sort of pupils, socio-economically
Parents may be more supportive	Parental pressure can be great
Smaller classes	Generally fewer opportunities for professional development
Not constrained by LA and DCSF bureaucracy	No automatic network with other local schools and advisers in the LA, particularly to help if things go wrong in your induction year
Don't have to teach the NC and the national strategies	Teaching and curriculum may be more conservative; they don't get government-funded publications and resources automatically
More opportunity to coach sports teams	More extra-curricular activities expected
Longer holidays	No nationally agreed pay scale
Union activity is unusual	Union activity is unusual

Table 6.1   Teaching in independent schools

> I've found a reception job in a prep school. If I do induction there the head says that I'll have to guarantee to stay for three years to make the financial investment worthwhile – and if I leave before that time I'll have to reimburse them about £500.

Independent schools don't get government funding but still have to provide the 90 per cent timetable and all elements of support, monitoring and assessment if they are fulfilling the regulations. This can be expensive, but your school will be saving money on your salary as you'll be cheaper than an experienced teacher. By the way, look at what pay they're offering: independent schools don't have to stick to national pay scales. Some pay more, some don't.

Supply teaching

Thinking about supply? Tempted by the seductive day rate, the lack of planning, marking and assessing, or the going home at the same time as the kids and without giving another thought to the job? Well, you need to think a few things through. The pay sounds good. One hears of supply teachers costing £300 per day, but this figure is what agencies get. You'll get just a fraction of that and you won't be entitled to sick pay, holidays, pension or paid leave. And even if you work for all the 190 school days in a year (which would be unusual), you'll still need money to support you for 365 days. Most supply agencies are not charities – they're businesses that make profit and capitalise on staffing crises in schools by putting their prices up. Some are more exploitative than others, so shop around.

The workload is potentially lighter. Not having to write plans, reports and assessments may seem like Nirvana after teaching practice, but again, there are drawbacks. You'll be expected to follow the planning left for you by class teachers. Gone are the days when you could turn up with winning lessons from your own private repertoire. Working from a plan that isn't yours can be hard, so inevitably lessons don't go so well and you'll rarely get the buzz that comes from successful teaching. If you're in a school for any length of time, you'll be expected to slot into the same level of planning, assessment and reporting as permanent staff, so the workload will become comparable with theirs.

You may be scared at the thought of having to be responsible for the education of a whole class of children. This is a common feeling, which is probably made a whole lot worse by thinking about it too much. Although not accountable for a whole year's worth, you'll still be responsible for children's well-being and education on every day that you work – and that can be hard in a supply teacher role.

Some people do supply because they can't face the thought of having to cross another mountain, which is what they consider induction (probation in Scotland) to be. It's not a hurdle to be dreaded. You'll have a reduced timetable and someone in charge of supporting, monitoring and assessing you, which is very reassuring. However, supply teachers on induction can be neglected: 'I did two Induction terms on Supply. No paperwork at all was completed in the first term, no lessons were formally evaluated and I had no NQT meetings in the whole time I was there.'

In England, there are specific rules for NQTs on supply, but some agencies don't make them very clear. Remember these two rules:

- You can only do short-term supply for 16 months, starting from your first day's work. After that you must get a post where you can get induction, otherwise you are not allowed to teach in the maintained sector.
- If you're going to be in a school for a term, you must be on induction and the school has to support, monitor and assess you as it would any other NQT. You are entitled to 10 per cent non-contact time, which the local education authority funds. Make sure you know your rights and gently remind people about their responsibilities.

Agencies vary greatly in terms of the support they give. There are many that will ignore the fact that you are newly qualified and not even tell the school to which they are sending you. Some offer what they call induction, which is actually aimed mostly at teachers from abroad. A few look after NQTs, find them a term's position and offer some training. The fees that agencies pay you and the support they give vary enormously, so it's worth shopping around and registering with several – if you decide to do supply.

Supply has pros and cons: with short-term jobs you get to see a variety of schools and practices, and you gain a lot of classroom teaching experience very quickly – a real baptism of fire. Doing supply is tough for an experienced teacher, so the odds are stacked against a new one succeeding. Controlling children you don't know, who see a supply teacher as fair game, and in a school with unfamiliar systems, is hard – and teaching them something worthwhile may be impossible. So try to get a settled job as soon as possible so that you can get the induction support you need.

Moving between primary, secondary and special

Once you have QTS you can teach in any sort of school, in theory. Every year there are people who trained to teach secondary who decide that they really want to work in primary or vice versa, and those who want to work in special schools. Although these are options, it makes most sense to gain most experience in the sort of school that you have training and some experience in already.

Swapping between different sorts of school is not easy, and best done when you have more experience under your belt. Each is a big leap, even on the amount of subject knowledge you'll need to teach confidently, to say nothing of the different ways of working. It will obviously be harder to get a job in primary if you are trained to teach secondary and vice versa, because you'll be competing with people who have greater knowledge and experience than you. Primary schools will be looking for someone to teach the whole curriculum. They might feel tempted by someone who is a Maths or English specialist, but are unlikely to feel the same about someone with French or German. Secondary schools want people who can teach one subject to GCSE, if not A level. There are a few conversion courses, but experienced teachers are more likely to get places than NQTs, who might be deemed to be running away from something. For instance, if you have problems controlling secondary pupils, you'll probably find primary even harder.

It's risky to do the move in your induction year as you'll have to meet all the core standards, just the same as someone who has already met the very similar QTS standards in that age phase. For most people, meeting them is no problem, but for you it will be, as your training experience will be so different from your work in training. Remember, if you fail to meet the standards after three terms you'll be de-registered from the GTC and never allowed to teach in the maintained sector again. The fact that you're doing induction in a different sort of school to that for which you were trained would not be grounds for appeal if you choose that path.

You can do induction in a special school, and a small number of people do so, but remember that you have your whole career in which to specialise. There are plenty of children with special needs in mainstream schools and the experience of teaching children with the full range of abilities will be invaluable whatever you eventually decide to do. Teaching effectively in a special school requires a great deal. Most people go into them having developed their skills and gained experience in mainstream schools, which is why there is no initial teaching qualification for special education. It is also easier to go from a mainstream to special school than vice versa. So, for all these reasons, think carefully about going straight into special education. Perhaps spend a few years in mainstream –

you'll be classed as experienced then, and be a better proposition for employers.

What sort of school will suit you?

Having considered the whole gamut of big options, think about what sort of a school would suit you. Every time you visit a school and spend time in a classroom and in the playground, take a good look at what you see around you. It will help you work out the kind of school you want to work in.

Look out for:

- what kind of relationship there is between pupils and staff – is it formal or informal? Which do you feel more comfortable with?;
- behaviour management policies – are they positive enough? Are they too liberal and lacking in discipline? Different policies suit different schools. What do you feel comfortable with?;
- the balance between academic progress and pastoral priorities;
- staff workload – what sort of hours are teachers working and do they seem happy about workload?;
- staff professional development – how much is there?;
- the leadership of the school – every headteacher has their own style. Make mental notes of the style of headteacher you like to work for. The same goes for senior management and departmental heads;
- the other teachers – the staffroom tells you a lot about a school. Are they laughing at the antics of a notorious child, swapping anecdotes, groaning at the latest round of paperwork or what was said about teachers on Radio 4 this morning? Or are their heads stuck in marking books, ignoring each other? More importantly, is there conversation that involves life outside of school? Do they make you pay 10p for a cup of coffee or does someone offer you a choice of biscuits? Is there gossiping about colleagues behind their backs?

These little things tell you a great deal about the character of the school. Different teachers suit different schools. What doesn't feel right for you is a joy to another. And vice versa, of course. The difficulty is deciding what is right for you.

Where to look for a job

Don't let the teacher recruitment posters lull you into thinking that it'll be easy to get a teaching job for September. The job market is complex, with regional, subject and phase variations. Those pictures of enthralled learners are there to entice people to become teachers of shortage subjects like Maths and Science.

You can begin to get a feel for the job market even before you decide to apply. Read the adverts every week to get an idea of the kinds of teaching jobs going for your age range and your specialist subject. Is there a demand in the part of the country where you'd like to teach? If not, where are they? The job market varies across the country. Of the 20 authorities with the highest percentages of new teachers in 2008, 18 were in London; the other two were Luton in Bedfordshire and Sandwell in the West Midlands. Among the authorities with the lowest percentages, seven were in the North East (Howson, 2009). A sizeable number of people who gain QTS do not go straight into teaching. The latest DCSF statistics show that 23.5 per cent of teachers weren't teaching in the country eight months after qualifying in 2006.

Don't panic unduly. There will be lots of jobs advertised in April and May, and then in June after the cut-off date for employed teachers to hand in their notice.

Read the job pages regularly and you'll get to know the 'adspeak'; a 'challenging' school might be right up your street, or it could be your idea of hell. Choose somewhere where you can make the most of your induction year. Concentrate on jobs that ask for a class teacher or an MPS post, sometimes referred to as common pay spine (CPS) or teacher pay scale (TPS). The salary scales are explained later in this chapter. You don't want to go for anything with a TLR – a teaching and learning responsibility. They are for people with management responsibility, not new teachers.

Jobs that are suitable for NQTs will often say so. If an advert doesn't specify this, but the post seems to be appropriate for you, give the school a ring and ask. Some schools offer relocation and rent and mortgage subsidies. Bear in mind that these incentives are there because they find it hard to get teachers – there's no such thing as a free lunch. Get a feel for their staff turnover. A school with frequent ads probably has a high turnover. This could mean quick promotion for you, but it's more likely to mean an unstable and unhappy working environment.

There are many places where you might find out about a job. Advertising is expensive. Many schools find teachers more cheaply through word of mouth, by posting vacancies on their website and at training colleges, and through the LA.

National newspapers and their websites

The *Times Educational Supplement* (*TES*) is the biggest and most established. It is published every Friday. The *Independent* and *Guardian* have a smaller number of adverts. If you want to work in a school that subscribes to a particular faith, read the job adverts in that denomination's newspaper. If you register on the *TES* jobs section, you can get an email or a text message telling you as soon as a job fitting your requirements is advertised.

LA jobs bulletins

Many schools advertise locally as well as, or before, doing so nationally. You'll need to register directly with the human resources/personnel department or recruitment strategy manager to get sent these. However, not all schools will use this service, so keep an eye on national adverts too.

LA pools

Many LAs use a pool system for new nursery and primary teachers, and some also use these for secondary teachers. They vary – some put you through a rigorous interview process, others just add your details to a database so schools can select candidates for interview. Pools mostly advertise in January and interview by March, so the big advantage is that you get a job early on in a school which doesn't interview. The disadvantage is that the school chooses you rather than you choosing the school, but you can turn offers down and you'll be returned to the pool until you're fished out by the next school that's interested in you.

Informally

Some jobs aren't advertised. Vacancies are often filled by people who someone at the school knows or has heard of. This is the hardest circle to break into. Many schools will give jobs to people who have done teaching practices with them. Schools also pass on information about good trainees they've come across, so it's really important to make good impressions in all your dealings with staff in school. Headteachers aren't necessarily looking for someone who is a brilliant teacher, but someone who takes advice, makes progress, is enthusiastic and gets on with people.

It may be worth sending your CV, with an accompanying letter, to schools that you fancy working in. This isn't common practice and many schools will simply discard unsolicited requests, but I've known a few people who have got jobs this way.

The next chapter will look at the detail of how to get a job.

seven

Getting that job

- Finding out more
- Application form
- Interviews
- Contracts
- Salary

When you've found a job you like the look of, you need to act fast. Most applications have to be in within two weeks of the advert, and interviews are held about one week later. The first step is to ring for an application form and information about the job. Do this immediately – don't delay. For instance, the *TES* comes out on Fridays. You'll need to read it in the morning and ring for an application pack at lunchtime.

Finding out more

Once you've requested the application form, do some detective work. Look at a map. Is your journey going to be long and stressful? Are the pupils likely to be rather too close to your home for comfort? Ask around – teaching is an incestuous profession and you're bound to find someone who knows about the school. Where is it placed in the league tables? You should also read the latest Ofsted report at www.ofsted.gov.uk. Reports use a four-point grading system, so the words 'good' and 'outstanding' are used very precisely, so translate what they write to get an accurate picture:

1. outstanding
2. good

3. satisfactory
4. inadequate.

Look out for the sections on Teaching and Learning as well as Leadership and Management – a poorly led school will be hard to work in.

Visiting schools

It's worth trying to visit before applying or attending the interview, because if you have a bad gut feeling, applying for a post is a waste of everyone's time. Headteachers differ in how they react to visits. Many are happy to see you taking the application process seriously; others don't allow visits until people have been shortlisted because they'd be inundated; and a few discard applications from candidates who haven't bothered to visit. If the application pack mentions that applicants can make an appointment to look around the school, then this means they expect you to visit before interview – and won't shortlist those who don't.

But beware: it gives school leaders a chance to check you out as well as letting you have a gut reaction about a place. First impressions count and even though it's not a formal interview, remember that you're on show. Dress smartly and be friendly. Try to speak casually to any newish teachers to find out if they're happy and whether they've been treated well. Ask pupils and staff about the work they're doing and show that you're interested. Look at displays, peer through classroom doors and notice the way the pupils and staff conduct themselves. Find complimentary things to say about what you see. And then seize the golden opportunity to relate the first sentence of your personal statement to your visit. Something like, 'Having visited your school, I was impressed by … because this is something which I feel passionately about.'

Who knows what might happen? One candidate went to look at a school before applying for a job and while being shown around was asked whether he would accept a job at the school if offered. He said yes and later in the day was offered the job by telephone. He filled in the application form as a formality, didn't have to go through an interview and the next day the advert was taken off the LA website even though it was before the closing date! This is a true story – there are lessons to be learned.

Another new teacher got the first job she applied for through doing the whole process of visiting the school, posting a thank-you letter and then submitting a personalised application. Even though nerves got the better of her at the interview, which meant she didn't perform well, she got the job anyway – because she'd made such a great impression.

Application form

As soon as you get your application form, photocopy it. You need to perfect a rough copy before you complete the real form. Read through it to see the information it requires. Check the closing date and make sure you have plenty of time to contact referees, draft the form, write the personal statement, complete the form, check it and post it with plenty of time for them to receive it. The first application form you fill in will take a long time! Follow any instructions about sending photocopies, using black ink and dead-lines (potential employers will adhere to these!). Don't send a CV with your form unless you're asked to – you will have provided the information they want. Make sure it looks good: write neatly, whether by pen using a word-processor.

Referees

How many referees does it ask for? Normally you need to name two, so people tend to use their college tutor and the headteacher of the most recent teaching practice school. Remember to ask people's permission to put their names as referees and let them know when the closing date for applications is and when interviews might be. This will give them an idea of when they'll get the reference request so they can schedule the writing of it. Often schools expect a very quick turnaround, which puts referees under pressure, so the more you can do to ease this, the better. Check what contact details you should put on the form – sometimes college tutors prefer to have requests faxed to them via an administrator for speed. Send them a copy of your application form so they can see what you have written about, and decide what needs reinforcing, and what they can mention that you've left out.

Your personal statement

Your personal statement should be written specifically for each job you apply for, but it's good to prepare a general one that you can amend accordingly. If you're applying to a pool, refer to the named LA rather than the school. It will be used to assess whether you meet the person specification part of the job description, so pay special attention to this when you're drafting it. The specification might include wanting people with a commitment to:

- working with parents, celebrating pupils' special skills and talents, as well as tackling problems;
- contributing to school life and building effective relationships with all members of the school community;
- evaluating, reviewing and, as necessary, adapting your own teaching to maximise pupils' achievements;
- developing professional skills and knowledge through induction and continuing professional development.

Everyone requires good oral and written communication skills, but jobs often also require the ability to create a rich and safe learning environment for all pupils by:

- establishing high expectations and promoting purposeful learning;
- implementing effective classroom management and organisation;
- assessing the needs of individual pupils and accurately recording and reporting their progress;
- good planning based on the Foundation Stage or NC schemes of work, and information from the assessment of pupils' learning needs.

How well does this person meet the criteria about using a range of teaching strategies to maximise progress for all?

> Within lessons, I plan for extension and differentiation to challenge the more able while enabling weaker pupils to strengthen their basic understanding of the core concepts; I have tried to implement this through starters and extension worksheets.

Are you put off by the jargon and does the word 'worksheets' raise alarm bells? What about this one?

> In all lessons I strive to meet the differing needs of pupils within the class. A recent example of this would be when pupils were learning to write written speech. I had the children with general learning difficulties and EAL learning problems work with a T.A. to arrange the cut up parts of a piece of written speech into the correct layout and then write it out into their books. The normal achievers were instructed to change speech bubbles into written speech, while the high achievers were extended by being expected to think of and write responses to the speech.

Using an example is a great idea, but is this person good at explaining clearly? Do you wince at the term 'normal learners'? Is this a good response to show your understanding of equal opportunities?

> In the classes I have taught in, children have came from a variety of different backgrounds, and I feel its part of the teacher's duty to understand this, and to be mindful of their impact on the child and his/her learning & development.

How did you feel about the missing apostrophe in 'its' and the use of the '&'? What other equal opportunities issues should she have shown awareness of?

Your personal statement needs to convey that you meet the person specification for the job they are recruiting for. Jot down examples of how you meet each part of the person specification. You'll find that there are many examples that fit different parts, so you need to decide which to use and where.

Give examples of how you meet the specification. For instance, 'I have a clear understanding of the literacy and numeracy strategies' says little. Show how you have gained the skills and knowledge through a practical example:

> During my school experience I was able to start to develop and use skills that are necessary to be an effective classroom teacher. I used a range of teaching methods, including discussions, games, collaborative activities and the individual-focused tasks. I also made my own resources to help make the lessons interesting and relevant to the children. I tried to motivate and enthuse the children in their work by activities having positive outcomes and celebrating their achievements. I also defined specific learning intentions for each lesson. These factors all contributed to the establishment of a rich and purposeful learning environment. I also listened to and respected the children's thoughts and ideas, and provided support for those who required it, to help the children feel confident, positive and safe within the classroom environment.

When structuring your writing think of how to be helpful to the reader. Use the same headings or order as the person specification. Express yourself with care. Don't use too much jargon. Be relevant and concise, and don't include anything you can't back up at interview. If it's not on the person specification, then it's not likely to be relevant. Address any problematic issues (poor qualifications, gaps in employment) that the reader is likely to have picked up on in reading the information parts of the application form. Try to turn things to your advantage.

Your personal statement should cover no more than two sides of A4, and it should be word-processed – it's easier to read and looks professional. Proofread it, then get someone else to check it … and then check it again! I can't emphasise enough how off-putting any spelling or grammatical errors are in an application form. Read it out loud to yourself; unlike a CV, your personal statement is prose and it needs to read well. It will be this, more than the rest of your application form, which gets you that interview.

Finally, keep a copy and read it again just before your interview. Attach a short covering letter or email saying where you saw the ad, that you are newly qualified and that you look forward to discussing your application with them. Ask for a read receipt if you are sending it via email.

Before you send the application off, check that you haven't:

- got the name of the school or headteacher wrong;
- left blanks on the application form or gaps in employment history – you'll be assumed to have been in prison!;
- exaggerated your skills – they may come back to haunt you;
- made any spelling or grammar errors;
- copied even one sentence from someone else's application – plagiarism is a huge sin.

Check your bulk or spam email folders as well as your inbox for invitations to interviews. You should hear whether you've been shortlisted after a week or two, though there is much anecdotal evidence that this does not always happen. Usually, a couple of weeks' silence signals that you have not been shortlisted. A month-long pause is enough to let you know that all hope is gone. But your failure is compounded by a lack of manners on the part of the school that neglects to tell you that you have been unsuccessful.

Interviews

You've been offered an interview – how exciting, but how terrifying! Again, preparation will be the key. First, confirm your attendance straight away and with professionalism. These things matter. Try to visit the school before the interview even if you weren't able to do so before you applied. This gives you a huge insight about what is being looked for. Remember though, you're being judged even on an informal tour. Try to speak casually to any new teachers to find out if they seem happy and whether they've been treated well.

Not all schools will pay for travel and accommodation for long-distance applicants, so ask before the interview whether they reimburse or contribute to expenses. Some schools in far-flung parts put all candidates up in a hotel the night before. All these little touches give you an insight into what sort of organisation you're going to.

Appearance is really important. You've got to feel good and look the part. Wear smart clothes, but make sure you'll be comfortable. Take a file with your application form and statement, a portfolio of work from teaching practice (in case you get a chance to show them) and a copy of the most recent *TES*. You can read this while waiting. It will make you look professional and may come in handy in answering a question or two.

Think about what an interview panel is looking for. The advert may have said they want a 'dynamic teacher', but want they realistically want is someone that shows:

- professionalism;
- a sense of excitement about teaching;
- energy, intelligence, creativity;
- passion in their answers;
- thoughtfulness and reflection;
- a willingness to learn and improve;
- positive body language and smiles.

Possible interview formats

Interviews vary in how formal they are and how long they last. This would be a question to ask when you phone to accept the interview. If you're going via the pool system you might be interviewed by an LA adviser, headteacher and someone from human resources. If you're being interviewed by a school, the interview could take any number of forms – it just depends on the school, how well organised they are, how proactive their governors are, how many applicants they've got and how short-staffed they might be on the day. It's usually the headteacher, one or two governors and a head of department (HoD) or other member of staff. I've even known people who have thought they were having a pleasant little chat, only to be told that they have the job – the interview was so informal.

Interviews can take place over a whole day, with all shortlisted candidates together. These may include experienced teachers and internal candidates. Don't be intimidated. Tell yourself you're good, enthusiastic – and cheap! You're likely to get a tour of the school, maybe a group interview/discussion, hopefully lunch, and, if you're there for a whole day, you'll probably be asked to teach a class, observed by some or all of the interviewing panel. You'll then be interviewed individually.

Some schools think up challenging activities for you to do as part of the interview:

> I was interviewed for a primary one-year temporary post, music specialist preferred. I was given 15 minutes to prepare a 10-minute talk on the benefits of music in the curriculum and then had to write half a term's planning of a musical topic in 35 minutes, linking it to all the other areas of the curriculum with no literature or national curriculum to refer to.

Or you might have to give a five minute presentation on a topic such as:

> If there were no rules in the world of learning, what experiences would your pupils get during the day?

You may be asked to wait until they've made their mind up, in which case you'll probably have to sit in the staffroom with the other candidates until one is called in and offered the job. It really is grim.

You're on show all day long. Be friendly and relaxed with any other candidates. If you meet pupils or teachers, ask them about work they're doing and show that you're interested. Look at displays, through classroom doors, at the way the pupils and staff conduct themselves. Most importantly, find complimentary things to say about what you see. And ask yourself: can you imagine yourself working in this school?

Teaching at the interview

Teaching at the interview is ghastly. It's a ridiculous expectation of someone who is yet to complete a teacher training course and isn't qualified. Still, you need to be prepared.

Consider what the interviewers are looking for, and plan to give them what they want. Think about how you can show that you're professional; have a rapport with children and manage them well;

are enthusiastic; plan well; use effective teaching strategies; and reflect on learning and teaching. Give the interviewers a word-processed copy of your plan – check for spelling errors first. Make sure it has a clear learning objective, some useful motivating activities and clear differentiation. Keep the lesson simple and do it well. Bring your own (or borrowed) resources rather than assuming that the classroom will have them. Think of questions for the very able and for those with special needs. Make sure your behaviour management is as good as possible. Make lots of eye contact with the pupils, smile, and use praise to reinforce the behaviour you want. Act confidently, even if you're terrified.

Afterwards, reflect on the lesson honestly and intelligently, showing that you can assess pupil's answers, and think of ways to improve your teaching. No one expects you to be perfect, but your interviewers want to see that you're enthusiastic, and can approach and reflect on unfamiliar situations with verve. Oh, and be modest when it goes superbly – they are lovely children aren't they?

So, in summary, remember:

- people aren't looking for a super-lesson – keep it simple but do it well;
- don't carry on with your planned lesson if it's obviously at the wrong level – adapt and do your best;
- relate to the children – learn a few names, smile;
- plan thoroughly – bring copies of a well-presented plan for the observers;
- bring resources;
- afterwards, reflect on the pupils' learning – and yours – and say something positive about the children.

Interview questions

You're likely to be asked questions along these lines:

- Why do you want to work in this school?
- What makes a good classroom?
- Describe a lesson you've taught that went well.
- How would you handle some difficult behaviour? (They'll give you an example.)

- If a parent came storming across the playground, what would you do?
- What will your number-one priority be when you take up a full-time teaching post?
- How do you plan to keep up-to-date?
- How will you go about building up relationships with your teaching assistant?
- How would you ensure that all children are treated equally in your class? Bear in mind gender, race, class, disability, cognitive ability, language acquisition, etc.
- How would you like to work with parents?
- How do you approach planning and assessment?
- How do you exploit opportunities for literacy and numeracy?
- Would you accept the job if it was offered to you? You're expected to say yes!

You can plan answers to these sorts of questions, thinking of examples from your experience that you can use to bring yourself to life. For instance, when asked about how you'd manage some difficult behaviour, refer to a real example of something you've experienced or observed. You'll be asked about your experiences on teaching practice, so have relevant anecdotes to hand on all the issues listed above. Think about what the question is getting at. A question about a bad experience is not there to trick you into showing how awful you are, but how resilient you are – and this is a very important characteristic.

Make eye contact with whoever is asking you a question and make sure you address each member of the panel during the course of the interview, even the governor who makes notes but says nothing throughout. If you're stumped on a question, smile and ask them to repeat it. No one expects a new teacher to be perfect, but they do expect you to be enthusiastic, prepared to ride a steep learning curve, to reflect and improve and to approach unfamiliar situations with intelligence. Be reflective. If they raise a weakness, or ask you about something you're weak on, turn it into a positive: give an example of how you picked up an unfamiliar subject quickly, or how a disastrous teaching experience taught you valuable lessons in needing to be flexible/using positive behaviour management/keeping records and so on.

Sometimes you'll be asked wacky questions such as:

Name two objects that represent what you'd bring to the school.

This kind of thing is to test your creativity and ability to think on your feet. So how about answering:

A space-hopper because I'm fun with lots of bounce and I make people smile; and a teddy as I hope I'll be a source of comfort, cuddles, warmth and stability.

Tee hee! But don't let your guard down, make negative comments about any other schools and/or get too relaxed and say things you may regret, especially when the formal aspect is over.

You'll be asked if you have any questions. You do – and will have written them down – if you want to come across as bright and proactive. Ask about the school's professional development and induction support for new staff, their behaviour management policy, or something specific to the team you'll be working in. This isn't the time to ask about pay or something tiddly like whether you'll have a desk. If your questions have been answered during the course of the day/interview, then smile and explain what they were and that they've been answered, thank you.

Contracts

You will usually be offered the job on the day, after everyone has been interviewed, or that evening or the next day. The school will expect you to accept straight away. Asking prospective teachers, who are dazed and wrung out by the interview process, to make an instant decision may seem unfair and unnecessary, but headteachers want the best they can get and if their first choice ums and ahs, they'll take the person who came a close second. Say you'll accept, *subject to a satisfactory contract and salary*. Remember that phrase, say it again and again in your head: *subject to a satisfactory contract and salary*. They should be clear about whether the contract is permanent or temporary and about the salary they're offering you, along with arrangements for your induction. If they're not, check you're happy before you formally accept in writing to the school.

There has been a range of problems with contracts:

- not being given a written contract or job description;
- being given a temporary one;
- expected to do a different job to the one described in the advert;
- not being given the fair number of points on the salary scale;
- accepting a job without realising that the above would be issues.

Many NQTs are given temporary contracts for no good reason. This results in insecurity, inequality and low status. Clearly a large number of schools are discriminating against them. One school rarely renews NQTs' one-year contracts, preferring to get a new lot of cheap labour each year so they can keep their salary budgets down: a continuous supply of cannon fodder (Bubb *et al.*, 2005). Temporary contracts are not good and you should apply for permanent posts, unless you have very little choice and you really, really want the job. There are times when you might agree to something that you later regret, like this person:

Q: I applied for a Key Stage One job, but at the interview I was asked if I would consider foundation stage – only too keen, I agreed! I was offered the job and accepted. I've since been told the position is to be the nursery teacher. I have no experience in the nursery and I am now extremely worried about my induction year. Ideally I would like to get a KS1 position at a different school but where do I stand as I have already verbally accepted the job?

A: You've been put in an uncomfortable position, but need to solve the problem quickly before it affects you and the school too much. A verbal agreement is as legally binding as a written one. Having said that, a school won't want you to be unhappy and can't realistically do much about you reneging on it. Anyway, much of the fault lies with the school in not being clear about the post, so I think you should explain your concerns to the head as soon as possible, so that both of you have time to resolve the situation. Here are some things to say. The organisation and management of children, staff and parents requires a high level of maturity, experience and skill, which you do not have. While you would be interested in such a challenge in the future, you feel that such a role would be too much for you in your induction year and thus would require the school to provide a great deal of support. You thought you were being interviewed for a Key Stage 1 job, and really feel that this is where your strength lies. Ask whether there is any possibility that you could teach at KS1 (I'm sure teachers could be reallocated to classes). If there isn't, say that though you really want to work at the school you regret that you will have to look elsewhere.

Rejecting an offer

If you decide not to accept the job, be gracious and reject the offer as quickly as possible. You should always treat a school as you would like to be treated yourself. It's not professional, let alone legal, to accept a job offer and then change your mind for a better offer, unless you have a good reason, such as a sudden change in domestic arrangements. If you have to do this, let them know as quickly as possible, in writing, and explain the reasons why. Bad behaviour has a way of coming back to haunt you.

Being rejected

Not getting a job offer is a fact of life for most of us at some point in our careers, so don't take it to heart. This is the time to see an interview as good practice for the next one. Make the most of it as a learning experience. Reflect on what you did well and think about what you can improve on next time. When you've had a few interviews you can see that the questions are along similar lines. Wrack your memory and note down all the questions you can remember being asked. Then you can practise getting the perfect answer to questions on behaviour management, equal opportunities, etc. Don't forget to pepper your answers with real life examples from your supply teaching to bring your responses to life. Come across as enthusiastic and keen to learn. That can more than make up for a lack of experience.

Though it's painful, do ask for feedback so that you can learn from the experience. The bearer of this bad news may not be able to offer this immediately, in which case ask if you can have ten minutes of their time in the near future. If you're told in writing, ring the school and ask if a member of the panel could call you at a time convenient to them.

You need to persevere in the job hunt. If you don't get a job for the start of term, do supply teaching. This will give you rich experience to draw on in your interview, and is a great way of getting to know about jobs that are coming up. It also gets your name about so that when you apply for jobs, you have a good reputation to back up your assertions.

Salary

Teachers' pay is really confusing because there have been so many changes. If you want to keep up-to-date go to your employer's or union website. All NQTs are paid on the six-point MPS. Most people start on M1. You move up one point every September, subject to satisfactory progress. Late starters, part-timers and temporary teachers go up one point if they've been employed for at least 26 weeks during the year. You can start higher up the scale than M1 in recognition of 'relevant' experience, though this is interpreted differently by different schools. Once awarded, your position on the MPS can't be reduced even if you move schools, so it's important to negotiate the best starting point that you can as soon as you're offered a job. But you've got to be proactive about stating your case based on your previous experience of working with children or in a role deemed to be appropriate to teaching. There are no hard or fast rules to what you'll get as it's down to the discretion of school governing bodies. Basically, it's a lottery: the same person could get paid on M3 in one school but only M1 in another, which is a difference of £3,000.

Before you start planning how to spend your hard-earned cash, remember that you only get about two-thirds of your salary as take-home pay because there are deductions for:

- tax – 20 per cent of any money earned over the personal allowance of £6,035;
- national insurance – 11 per cent;
- pension (also called superannuation) – 6.4 per cent (and your employer contributes 14.1 per cent to it);
- GTC membership – £33 per year.

eight

Life in school

- Before you start
- Your classroom
- Planning
- Parents
- Reports

Life in school moves at a very fast pace and you need to hit the ground running by getting off to a good start. This chapter covers some basics, such as knowing how the school works, setting up the classroom, coping with planning, parents and writing pupil reports.

Before you start

The induction process starts as soon as you are appointed. You should get a job description, contract, arrangements for salary payments and pension contributions and procedures for sick leave. You may be asked to go for a medical. You should be sent documentation that will enable you to get a feel for the school. This would include the following, though items might be prioritised or staggered to avoid overload:

- school prospectus;
- staff handbook or something that details things such as how to complete the register, school and playground rules, planning formats;
- teaching and support staff list – professional and staff-room names, classes taught and responsibilities;

- administration staff list – professional and staff-room names and responsibilities;
- curriculum policies;
- curriculum schemes of work relevant to your teaching;
- other policies (health and safety, safeguarding, bullying, etc.);
- timetable;
- diary of school events.

The initial visit

The headteacher should arrange, where possible, for you to visit the school to familiarise yourself with the environment and colleagues, and to meet the class(es) you will be teaching. You should leave the school feeling full of enthusiasm, with lots of information and secure in the knowledge that you will be supported. Careful planning will ensure that you get the most out of the visit. Ask whether all the people you think you'll want to talk to will be available. Everyone will be busy and unlikely to be able to spare you much time. Write a list of all the things you want to know and tick them off when you've found the answer. Make another list of anything that you want to come away with.

I have, however, known people to return from these visits so worried that they speak of not signing contracts. Their impressions of the school gained at interview have been contradicted by talking to jaded teachers, and seeing pupils behaving badly. Every year, there are one or two NQTs who do not turn up at their school or who leave after the first week. Remember that you're probably seeing the school at its least desirable: at the end of term, with exhausted teachers and demob-happy pupils. It will be better at the start of the school year.

You should try to:

- meet the pupils;
- get a feel for the standard of work of the pupils (high, average and low attainers) that you will be teaching;
- look at records;
- see the classroom;
- look at resources in your classroom;
- look at resources in the school;

- look at the local environment;
- become familiar with routines and procedures;
- meet teaching, administration and support staff, especially those with whom you'll be working;
- spend some time with key people:
  - the headteacher and deputy headteacher;
  - teachers who know the pupils you will be teaching;
  - induction tutor;
  - teachers with whom you will be planning;
  - year and/or phase group coordinator or HoD;
  - special educational needs coordinator (SENCO);
  - support staff with whom you will be working;
  - premises officer;
  - secretary.

At some time before or during the first week, the induction tutor needs to agree a programme with you based on your strengths and areas for development from training and your present teaching context.

Timetable

Check your timetable to see that you have your 10 per cent reduced timetable and 10 per cent time for planning, preparation and assessment (PPA). If you are a secondary teacher, check that you are teaching the subjects that you applied to teach, and not extras.

Schools vary in the amount of cover they ask NQTs to do. In some, they're used only as a last resort. In others, their goodwill and enthusiasm are shamelessly exploited. Unfortunately, you can't refuse to cover, though lots of schools try not to use NQTs, at least for the first term or two. Certainly don't let cover eat into your reduced timetable. That doesn't mean that you can't be asked to cover for absent colleagues in your free periods, but remember the notion of 'bankable cover'. If you're called upon to do cover, the time can be 'banked' and repaid at a later date. If you earmark free periods for induction and spend them on professional development then they're less likely to get taken away.

Your classroom

One of the hardest things that you'll have to do as a teacher is also the first – set up the classroom. It really is exciting. You have your own classroom at last! Try to visit the school at the end of term, before you start. Have a good look around at the classroom you'll be in and what it's got: photos might be useful. Look at other rooms and resources in the school. Perhaps draw diagrams and take photos, because things will look very different at the start of the school year. You really need to go into school in the last week of the holiday before you start. Find out when the building will be open and teachers allowed in. You'll probably be confronted with a pile of furniture in the middle of the room – a ghastly sight! Don't panic – think about how other classrooms you've been in have been arranged. Dig out those diagrams and photos from teaching practice. The physical environment is crucial, but a well-arranged and organised room needs planning, physical effort and time.

The position of electrical sockets will determine where you put computers, tape recorders and overhead projectors. When you've got these in position you can build up the rest of the room. Make sure you've got a desk to work at (don't ruin your back by crouching over the children's tables after school) and shelves to store your files, etc. A lockable drawer or cupboard is useful for keeping things like money and staple guns in.

Look at the furniture you've been given. Are there items that you don't need? Often new teachers are given cast-offs. Look around other classrooms to check that you have a fair allocation. Are there enough tables and chairs? Find out the maximum number of children you'll have in the room and then have a couple spare in case of new arrivals, needing to split people up or being sent children from another class. Remember to allow space for moving around and for other adults who might be working in the room, and any equipment for children with special needs.

Think about how you're going to teach when deciding how to arrange the tables. How often do the pupils work collaboratively in groups? Everyone needs to see you when you're whole-class teaching, so where are you going to stand? Where is the white-board? Popular arrangements include rows, horse-shoes and clusters of fours or sixes. Choose whatever you think is going to work best for you and the children rather than slavishly following what other teachers do.

There are huge benefits to flexible seating arrangements. For instance, one teacher has two layouts for her class of 29 children. Her basic arrangement is a double horse-shoe, with tables laid out into a big and a small U shape, and a table for group teaching. This is used for whole-class teaching, paired and individual work. There's sufficient space between the two Us for her to move comfortably around and work in front or behind any child. She rearranges the tables for collaborative activities, usually in science and history. They are moved to form five grouped sets. A team of six children does this just before breaktimes and it only takes a minute.

Display

The number of bare display boards in your room may fill you with blind panic. Unless they're painted or already covered, ask an assistant to put up backing paper and some posters until the pupils do some displayable work. You may be in a school where support assistants do all the displays for you. Even so, you'll probably need to tell them what you want. Getting ideas for displays can be hard, so keep photos of other displays, look around the school and in books and ask others for inspiration. There are always people in school who love displays and will be more than happy to help you. In fact many, including myself, find it a really creative, relaxing and rewarding part of teaching. Ask for help. Here are some tips that new teachers have shared:

- Laminate labels that can be used again, especially ones with pupils' names on.
- Involve the pupils in writing labels, mounting work and finding artefacts.
- Pre-cut paper (to be smaller than A4) for pupils to work on so that it can be mounted on A4 paper and not need trimming.
- Have permanent displays that only need occasional additions.
- Attach some card or a coin to your staple gun so that the staple doesn't go all the way in to the board, but is slightly raised for easy removal. That way, work, labels and backing paper won't get torn.

- Save artefacts for displays that you are likely to repeat.

Resources

Have you got everything that you need to teach your age group? Ask your induction tutor for missing items. Organise resources to minimise fuss and wasted time. Everyone should know where they're kept and the procedures for getting things out and putting them away. Think hard about the particularly troublesome things such as:

- things brought from home, e.g. packed-lunch boxes, bags, PE kits;
- pencils and pens, sharpeners, rubbers, scissors;
- exercise books, worksheets, unfinished work;
- reading folders, homework.

Procedures

A good activity for the first day of term is to discuss with the pupils what the rules for the smooth running of the class should be. Phrase them positively: 'We will listen when an adult is talking.' Display them centrally, perhaps with illustrations and then refer to them continually: 'Well done, you're doing rule 3.' Think through procedures for moving from the carpet to tables, lining up, going to the toilet, tidying, etc. These need planning, training, practice and reinforcement, particularly for difficult times of the day.

Don't worry if things don't work straight away. You'll need to adjust the arrangement of the room and procedures so that they work for your class. This takes time and effort, but it's worthwhile. You will be able to teach more effectively and the children will learn more, so the classroom will be a happier, more productive place.

Activity

Watch *Primary NQTs: From One Thing to Another* (www. teachers.tv/video/3070).

How do the teachers in the programme manage transitions? What ideas can you try?

Planning

Planning is an essential aspect of teachers' work. All teachers need to plan what they will teach and how they will teach it, but spending excessive amounts of time on long, detailed plans does not necessarily lead to better teaching and learning. In Chapter 4 there are some ideas for lesson planning that you might want to look at, but one of your challenges will be to teach well without having to rely on such detailed plans as the ones you wrote on teaching practice.

Making resources

Teachers spend a great deal of time making resources, but think about 'fitness for purpose'. Is it worth spending time on resources in terms of:

- what children learn;
- how long they use the resource for;
- how many times the resource is going to be used;
- what else you could be doing?

Sometimes professional pride makes you do an unnecessarily perfect job. Keep things simple. Using ICT to make resources and worksheets will normally save time – and is useful as a way to share and store worksheets so that they can be adapted for future use – but sometimes handwritten versions can be quicker. Somebody (in your school or at a neighbouring one) probably has the resources you're looking for, so ask around before you need them. Share resources with teachers of the same year group. Organise a system for keeping resources so that you can find them next time you teach that particular topic.

Planning for support staff

In your first year you'll have to manage the work of other adults, as well as the learning of the pupils. As a group, support staff are really unsung heroes who have a massive effect on children and teachers. Most support staff are of high quality, but some can prove challenging to manage. Table 8.1 has some issues identified by new teachers, with a few suggestions for solutions.

It's important to know exactly what they're paid to do and then discuss the nitty gritty of that. What's their job description? What are you happy for a TA to do? For instance, as a teacher you can ask and expect TAs to put up displays, but some teachers can't bear to see a display done less than perfectly. Certainly, someone in the school should be able to do photocopying, but that might not be your TA's role.

You need to work as a team and be completely consistent in your rules and routines and back each other up. Some children

Issue	Ideas/solutions
Being unsure of the additional adult's role.	Find out exactly what they are paid to do. For instance, some special needs assistants are funded to work with individual pupils.
Not sure when they are going to be in the class.	Find out exactly when they're coming and make sure they know that you're expecting them.
Not wanting to ask them to do menial tasks.	Again, look at their job description. Most are happy to help out.
Some do too much for the children and encourage over-dependence.	Model the sort of teaching you want. Don't be afraid to mention concerns – they haven't benefited from training like yours and so are usually more than pleased to be given advice.
Some have little control over the children.	Again, model how to manage behaviour. Speak to their line manager if it's a big problem.
Some can take over the class.	This is very tricky. Speak to them about the need to establish yourself as the teacher, but otherwise get advice from your induction tutor.
Some talk when the teacher has asked for everyone's attention.	Theatrically or humorously emphasise that you need *everyone's* attention.
Some don't do quite what you've asked them to.	Explain, model, write instructions; speak to them about your concern.
Some are stuck in their ways and do not like new ideas and practices.	Tricky. Try to get them on your side by asking for their advice and their patience in trying things out.
Planning for them, when they do not turn up.	Make sure they and others know how much you depend on and value them. Make a fuss if they're taken away too often.

Table 8.1 Problems with support assistants

need loads of attention, so using a TA to give that means that you can get on with teaching. The key to a good partnership includes good communication, time to talk, clear roles and expectations and respect. They make the most difference, when they know exactly what's what. But often they are under-directed. Sometimes TAs aren't sure where to sit, so just make things clear. Try to explain the rationale behind things – remember, they haven't benefited from the training and educational theory that you have.

If there are things that are bugging you, think through how to tackle them. Certainly don't let them niggle away at you or one day you'll snap and probably ruin your relationship. Find out what they're comfortable and experienced in – and what they're not. Don't pick on someone to sing a verse of a song in front of the class unless you've briefed them and certainly don't wait for the school trip to realise that they have a scarily laid back approach to crossing roads.

Confident TAs can help deliver the lesson. Examples might be echoing the teacher by repeating, rewarding or refining teaching points, e.g. repeating or rephrasing instructions for pupils who are slow to respond: 'That's right – look for the speech marks.' The most obvious benefit of TAs is the presence of an extra pair of eyes (and ears) for:

- observing individual pupils;
- noting who 'can' and who 'can't';
- picking up emergent issues;
- comparing notes and giving feedback to the teacher.

How do you brief them before a lesson? The format in Figure 8.1 could be used. It really helps if they're involved in planning because it not only means that they'll understand what you and they are doing, but why – and they're bound to have some good ideas, especially if they're working with a child who has special needs. Even marking could be done by TAs if they're fully briefed and trained on how to do so and how to fit in with the whole school policy and your style. Investing time in them pays huge dividends – and when you build up trust they can give you valuable feedback on your teaching.

Name: Lesson and time:
What to do while I am whole-class teaching: Introduction: Plenary:
Pupils to support: Where and when:
Activity: What the pupils should do: What I would like you to do: What I want them to get out of it: Things that they will need:
How did they get on?   *Thank you!*

Figure 8.1   Plan for an additional adult

Parents

Dealing with parents is challenging because it calls for skills that you probably had little need to develop during teaching practices. Parents/carers can be very difficult to cope with – especially if they know that you are an NQT. You need to fill them with confidence (something that you may not yet feel you possess!) that their child is in safe hands educationally. Parents/carers want to know that you will be fair, not pick on their child, keep order so that their child can get on with their work and teach well to enable progress to be made. They will also probably expect you to know their child well. Tips for dealing with parents/carers are:

- look confident;
- dress appropriately;
- act particularly professionally and confidently when parents are around;
- in all dealings maintain a quietly assertive, polite and confident manner;
- maintain a professional distance no matter how well you get to know the parents;
- be honest though tactful;
- give clear messages – avoid educational jargon;
- listen to what they have to say;
- follow up concerns that they have;
- do whatever you say you will do;
- refer significant issues to more senior teachers.

Your school may ask you to keep a record of both formal and informal contacts with parents/carers. This can be used when you initiate contact over problems such as lateness, homework, behaviour, or more positive things such as a particularly good piece of work or improvement in behaviour.

Parents' evenings

Parents' evenings are stressful, even for experienced teachers. Many NQTs find the thought terrifying. Everyone feels the same way and everyone survives. You should get some help from your induction tutor. Someone needs to talk you through your specific school's procedures and to warn you of any parents who are known to be difficult – and the best way to deal with them. Ideally, arrange to sit in on another teacher's interview with a parent to see how they structure it.

You'll feel more confident if you prepare. What is the aim of the consultation? Is it for you to meet parents, or to set targets and discuss progress? Whatever it is, make sure that the parents are clear and that you're prepared. Spend some of your 10 per cent reduced timetable getting ready.

Write notes about each child, identifying strengths and areas for development socially and academically (see Figure 8.2). It's useful to ask the children what they think you'll say. Their understanding

Pupil
Work – strengths
Illustrative piece of work:
Work – weaknesses
Illustrative piece of work:
Areas to work on:
Social, behaviour and attitude
Targets:
Parents' comments:
Date:

Figure 8.2 Notes for parents' evenings

of how they're doing is essential. Keep the notes on separate pieces of paper so that people can't see what you're going to say about any other children. Check the last written report so that you know what the parents have been told before. You'll probably be reinforcing what has already been said, but if you're planning to say something that contradicts previous messages, make sure you have hard evidence to back it up. If you can predict what issues parents might raise, think of some answers. Take care with what you say and how you say it, as it'll all get analysed and talked about afterwards. Be thoroughly professional and tactful: if you think someone's lazy then say that the pupil has not really worked hard this term, but that there is still time to turn this around.

Plan the timetable of meetings carefully, giving yourself breaks where possible – but don't rely on having any gaps as you'll probably run over time with some parents. Organise your teaching for that day and the day after to be fairly easy going. You won't have the time or energy to do marking or planning after a parents' evening.

You are being judged as much as the pupils (especially as a new teacher), so make sure your personal presentation does you credit. Bring a spare set of smart clothes to change into and allow time to freshen up. Arrange a table and some adult-sized chairs. Ensure that marking is up-to-date and everything appears organised, especially any work that is going to be looked at. If you're in a primary school try to have something from every child on display. Keep anything to hand that you might possibly need, such as examples of work, records and curriculum documents. Lastly, have a supply of drinks and nibbles to keep you going. Try to look confident – even if you don't feel it. Remember that most parents will be nervous too.

Activity

Watch *Secondary NQTs: Reporting to Parents* (www.teachers. tv/video/2710).

This shows two new teachers coping with parents' evening and writing reports. What can you learn from this?

The meeting itself

Make sure that parents know how long they've got with you – this is normally only about ten minutes, but both you and they will want longer. Keep a clock or watch on the table so that you and they can keep to time, although this is very hard to do. You need to manage the time really well – try to be ruthlessly efficient. Trouble will brew if people are kept waiting too long. You can always suggest that parents who need longer make an appointment to see you on another occasion.

Work out a structure for the meeting, such as:

1. Introduction: 'Hello, you must be X's mum' or 'You've come to talk about X' (don't use people's last name unless you're sure of it, can pronounce it and know their title – the potential for offence and wasted time is too great).
2. Headline: 'X has settled in well and is making progress.'
3. Strengths (social and academic): 'I'm particularly pleased with ...' (have some work that illustrates your point).
4. Area for improvement (social and academic): 'However, X still needs to work on ...' (again, have some illustration).
5. Parents' views: 'How do you think X is doing? Do you have

any concerns?' (You could ask this after your headline but you'd risk losing time for your agenda. If you know what they are likely to raise, plan a response. Make a note of their concerns.)

6. Parental help: 'Could you make sure X practises....'
7. Conclusion: (look at watch, stand up, offer hand to shake) 'Well, thank you for coming. If you have concerns in the future please let me know.'

If you can predict parents who might be difficult, arrange for another member of staff to be around, perhaps bringing you a cup of coffee at a prime time. Have a list of your appointments and tick when you have seen parents. This should stop you getting confused and talking about the wrong child – it has happened!

You'll feel a great sense of achievement when it's over, so celebrate with a glass of something nice in a hot, relaxing bath.

Reports

I don't want to alarm you, but writing reports is probably the most important thing you will do as a teacher. Reports are read over and over again by many people, passed around families and friends and kept for posterity. I bet yours are still in some safe place at home.

Even though you may think much of the other paperwork you do has little purpose, reports matter. What you write will last forever, and may come back to haunt you. Your report on a nine-year-old who 'can identify and keep the beat in a piece of music' might seem embarrassingly like damning with faint praise when he's a famous musician featured on *This is Your Life*.

Reports also form part of the induction standards you must show you have reached by the end of your first year in teaching. These say you must liaise effectively with pupils' parents or carers through informative oral and written reports on pupils' progress and achievements, discussing appropriate targets and encouraging them to support their children's learning, behaviour and progress.

Writing reports is time-consuming for all teachers, but for the newly qualified it can seem a mammoth task. Don't be deceived by computer programs that promise to do it all for you – the process still takes ages. Although you will have had a session on reports during your training, you will have had little opportunity to develop this skill – and it's a skill that takes time and practice. Speak to your induction tutor about how much detail to put in. I know of schools that go for something quite minimalist, but others require a lengthy paragraph on each subject. The structure varies, too. Some have statements about the curriculum covered by the whole class, so you need to make comments only about each individual's overall progress.

Build up a bank of useful phrases, particularly ones that express criticisms in a positive way. Read last year's reports to get a feel for style. Talk to other teachers to see how you can be honest but positive. A phrase such as, 'She produces good work when she applies effort' sounds so much better than, 'She's bone idle.' Remember that even your most dreaded pupil is someone's baby. Think of the overall message you want the pupil and parents to get before you get bogged down in detail. Having up-to-date records will help. Ask pupils to provide a self-assessment – what they are good at, have made progress in, have enjoyed, need to improve. Their views are usually accurate.

Write succinctly. Try to make specific contextual comments to give a flavour of the individual. Reports should be clearly understood by parents or carers, so avoid educational jargon. This is easier said than done when it comes to talking about place value in Maths, for instance. Start with positive comments before introducing negative ones. Make clear what the pupil has to do to improve.

Draw up a timetable for writing your reports. Pace yourself – you can't knock them out in a rush. If you write yourself an objective about reports, you can justifiably spend some of your 10 per cent reduced timetable writing them. Choose a straightforward child to write about first to get into the swing, but show it to a senior member of staff for approval before doing the rest. One NQT wrote all his reports at half-term but had to redo them all because they weren't good enough.

Build rewards into your timetable – anything to make you stick to it. Believe me, the sense of achievement when they're all done is fantastic!

Report-writing checklist:

- Draw up a timetable of when you're going to write your reports.
- Speak to others about how they go about it.
- Read old reports to get a feel for style and useful phrases.
- Write a straightforward one first.
- Use some of your 10 per cent release time to write them.
- Ask the children to do a self-assessment.
- Think of the overall message.
- Write succinctly and avoid jargon.
- Start with positive comments.
- Phrase negatives positively.
- Suggest what the pupil has to do to improve.
- Get them checked by a senior member of staff.

Ask yourself:

- Have I commented on all the necessary areas?
- Have I made any spelling or grammatical mistakes?
- Will the parent/carer understand it?
- Does it give a clear, accurate picture?
- Is it positive? Are weaknesses mentioned?

Life in school can seem like a whirlwind. Induction exists to help you through so that you end your first year by being the best you can be. The next two chapters deal with this: the first focuses on the rules while the second looks at how to make the most of your entitlement.

nine

Understanding induction

Differences between England, Scotland and Wales

The rules in England

Roles and responsibilities

The induction tutor

Becoming a really good teacher is like a long journey. Some parts will be smooth and fast flowing, others stressful and full of traffic jams – but you'll be making progress all the time, even if the congestion you meet reduces your speed to only five miles per hour. Induction and all professional development can help you pick up speed in your journey. If you don't take advantage of what it has to offer it won't be the end of the world. You'll make some progress just through experience – but you'll only be travelling slowly. Using all the help available to develop professionally will get you speeding along at a comfortable 30 mph. But beware of the temptation to speed or you might crash. You'll burn out or get promoted to positions for which you are insufficiently experienced and credible – and which cause you stress.

Differences between England, Scotland and Wales

The regulations and support covering the first year of teaching vary depending on which country you work in. England has had statutory induction since May 1999; Scotland changed from a two-year to a one-year probationary period in August 2002; and Wales made induction compulsory in September 2003. Table 9.1 compares the rules for the three countries. The standards that new

	England	Scotland	Wales
First year called	Induction	Probation	Induction
You're known as a	NQT	New teacher	NQT
Entry qualifications	Degree + QTS	BEd or degree + PGCE, not GTP or RTP	Degree + QTS. Speaking Welsh helps but is not essential
Arrangements started	May 1999	August 2002	September 2003
Lead organisation	General Teaching Council for England	General Teaching Council for Scotland	General Teaching Council for Wales
Timetable reduction	10%	30%	10%
Who looks after you	Induction tutor	Supporter	Induction tutor
Induction tutor time	None	10%	None, but extra funding
Judged against	Core standards	The Standard for Full Registration	The End of Induction Standard
Assessment	Three times	Twice	Three times
How to get a job	You find it	You are placed in a school	You find it
Time limit between QTS and induction	None	Have to do probation straight away	Five years
Short-term supply	16 months		Five years

Table 9.1 The first year: differences between England, Scotland and Wales

teachers in each country have to meet can be found on the relevant GTC website. This chapter concentrates on English regulations, but here is some key information about Wales and Scotland.

Scotland

All teachers must be registered with the GTCS to get a post in a school. New teachers are given provisional registration and have to do one year's probation to meet the Standard for Full Registration. People who train in Scotland are guaranteed a one-year new teacher post. They are allocated to one of the LAs and then to a school. New teachers can't choose a school. The placement is for one year, but there is no guarantee that people will be able to stay afterwards. Deferment isn't possible, except on such grounds as needing maternity leave. People who trained outside Scotland can do probation if they have a provisional registration with the GTC, but they aren't guaranteed a new teacher post. They can take longer to complete probation.

New teachers are given a very generous 70 per cent timetable – the rest is for professional development, which consists of core experiences, which the authorities will organise, and individual activities. Each new teacher has a special 'supporter' who has a role similar to the induction tutor in England. This person has half a day each week to meet and observe the new teacher. Assessment forms are completed twice per year. The standards on which new teachers are judged cover rather more extensive areas than those in England and build on those standards for Scottish initial training. For more and up-to-date details go to www.gtcs.gov.uk.

Wales

Wales was slow to make induction statutory (September 2003), but the distinctive feature is that induction is seen as part of early professional development (EPD) over the first three years. This is already in place in Northern Ireland. NQTs are assessed on induction standard (see www.gtcw.gov.uk). Anyone failing will be given the opportunity to retake induction: this is certainly a softer approach than England's 'zero tolerance of failure'.

The rules in England

England has the most vacancies for NQTs and the most embedded induction arrangements. NQTs are protected from 'unreasonable' demands such as curriculum coordination and especially demanding behaviour problems. They have an individualised programme of support, monitoring and assessment from an induction tutor and objectives are set to help meet the standards for the induction period. There are assessment meetings and reports at the end of each of the three terms. However, people who fail induction in England are never allowed to teach in maintained schools or non-maintained special schools again. They cannot retake induction, and extensions are only allowed in special cases such as more than 30 days of illness. The good news is that only 74 out of 36,928 failed in the first three years – and a few successfully appealed against failure. So the odds of you failing are remote.

What the induction period consists of

The induction period lasts for one school year, which in most cases means that it will start in September and end in July. This is three terms or the equivalent. Thus, if you only work two-and-a-half days per week, your induction period will last for six terms. It should start as soon as you start work on a regular timetable for at least one term, even if this is in the middle of a term.

The induction guidance says:

> The induction period will combine an individualised programme of monitoring and support, which provides opportunities for NQTs to develop further their knowledge, skills and achievements in relation to the Standards for the award of QTS, with an assessment of their performance.
> (Department for Children, Families and Schools, 2008)

The key words are: monitoring, support and assessment. In practice this means that there is an entitlement for NQTs that should last throughout their induction period. The support, monitoring and assessment must be balanced over the year.

The NQT entitlement

Some NQTs get more than they are strictly entitled to, but about one-fifth do not get all that they should have. You are entitled to the following:

1. A job description that does not make unreasonable demands (see below).
2. An induction tutor.
3. Meetings with the induction tutor.
4. The Career Entry and Development Profile (CEDP) discussed by the NQT and induction tutor.

5. Objectives, informed by strengths and areas for development to help NQTs improve so that they meet the standards for the induction period.
6. A 10 per cent reduction in timetable – this will be half a day off per week or the equivalent number of free periods.
7. A planned programme of how to spend that time, such as observations of other teachers.
8. At least one observation for each half term, with oral and written feedback, meaning a minimum of at least six per year.
9. An assessment meeting and report towards the end of each term.
10. Procedures for NQTs to air grievances about their induction provision at school and a 'named person' to contact at the Appropriate Body (AB), usually the LA.

However, there are many confusions about and contraventions of the induction policy. Here are answers to frequently asked questions.

Where can I do statutory induction?

These regulations only apply to England, Guernsey, Jersey, Gibraltar and the Isle of Man and Services schools in Germany and Cyprus. Qualifications such as QTS and induction in each country in the EEA are recognised in England and vice versa. Teachers who qualified in England after May 1999 but teach outside the EEA will have to do induction when they return.

Are there any schools in England in which I can't do induction?

Yes, you can't do induction in a Pupil Referral Unit, or a school under special measures unless Her Majesty's Inspectorate (HMI) says you'll be well supported. You can only do it in an independent school if they have an AB – the LA or Independent Schools Council Teacher Induction Panel (ISCTIP).

The school says it can't afford to give me 10 per cent release time.

It's a statutory duty of headteachers to give teachers on induction only a 90 per cent timetable. Your headteacher has no choice in the matter.

My half-day for induction is often cancelled because of staff sickness.

There will inevitably be times when this happens, but your induction time should be protected as far as possible and, if missed, should be made up at some other time.

What happens if I fail induction?

If your headteacher and LA think that you do not meet the induction standards, you won't be allowed to teach in a maintained school or non-maintained special school in England. You would be able to teach in an independent school or work as a private tutor and abroad, outside of the EEA. Your qualified teacher status isn't taken away.

Who must complete the statutory induction period?

Everyone who qualified after May 1999 has to complete an induction period to work in state schools in England. Their induction year starts as soon as they have a teaching job for a term or more in the maintained sector.

Is there a time limit between qualifying and starting induction?

No. You can also take a break after the first or second of the three terms in the induction period. The only thing that has a time limit is short-term supply work: 16 months.

Everyone says I'm doing well, so my induction has fizzled out.

Induction is statutory for all NQTs. Even the very successful have the right to be challenged so they become even more effective teachers. Be proactive in asking for meetings and observations.

The school is in crisis – priorities are elsewhere, not on us.

It will be particularly hard to complain to the headteacher and LA in this situation, but all the more important. If you are not getting the support you need, you won't teach effectively and the children's learning will suffer further.

Roles and responsibilities

It's essential that everyone is clear about roles and responsibilities. You should take an active role in all aspects of the induction process. In particular, you should:

- work with your induction tutor to analyse your strengths and weaknesses as a basis for setting objectives for professional development;
- take part in planning your induction programme, including the identification and review of objectives to help you meet the core standards;
- engage fully in the programme of monitoring, support and assessment that is agreed with the induction tutor, taking increasing responsibility for your professional development as the induction period progresses;
- be familiar with the core standards and monitor your own work in relation to them;
- raise any concerns you have about the content and/or delivery of your induction programme.

Being aware of your rights will help you in any area of concern. Use this book and the induction guidance (Department for Children, Families and Schools, 2008) to back up any points that you need to make. Knowing the AB, headteacher and induction tutor's responsibilities will also help you.

The appropriate body

Schools need to have an AB to which they send reports and which has a quality-assurance role. All LAs act as ABs. In independent schools, the AB will be either the LA for the area in which the school is situated or the ISCTIP. The induction guidance outlines what is expected of appropriate bodies. Their specific statutory duties are:

1. Ensuring that headteachers and governing bodies are aware of and capable of meeting their responsibilities for monitoring, support and guidance.

2. Ensuring headteachers are capable of undertaking rigorous and fair assessments of NQTs.
3. Making the final decision about whether an NQT meets the standards for the completion of the induction period and communicating their decision to NQTs, schools and the GTC.
4. Keeping records and assessment reports on NQTs.
5. Providing a named person for NQTs to contact if they are unhappy with schools' support, monitoring and assessment.
6. Extending the induction period in exceptional circumstances.

So, what can new teachers do when their school doesn't play by the rules? In practice, not a lot. Who is going to complain about their assessor – the headteacher or induction tutor – when these people can recommend a fail? The induction system assumes that all headteachers and LAs know what they're doing and are reasonable people. Unfortunately, some NQTs wouldn't see it like that!

The headteacher

The headteacher has key responsibilities to:

1. ensure that each NQT in their school is provided with an appropriate induction programme, in line with national arrangements;
2. make a recommendation to the LA, based on rigorous and fair assessment procedures, as to whether the NQT has met the core standards;
3. designate an induction tutor for each NQT, and ensure that this person is adequately prepared and is able to work effectively in the role;
4. ensure that any duties assigned to you are reasonable;
5. ensure that you are provided with a timetable representing no more than 90 per cent of the average contact time normally allocated to more experienced teachers in the school, and ensure that the time released is protected, is distributed appropriately throughout the induction period and is used to support your professional development from the very outset of the induction period;

6. inform the LA if you are at risk of failing to meet the standards and observe your teaching.

Unreasonable demands

The induction circular says that teachers in their induction year should not be given a job description that makes unreasonable demands. Some NQTs have a job that contravenes almost all the guidance, such as shown in Table 9.2.

NQTs should have a job that...	The NQT's experience
Does not demand teaching outside the age range and subject(s) for which the NQT has been trained.	Compliance
Does not present the NQT on a day- to-day basis with acute or especially demanding discipline problems.	Discipline was a significant problem in the school. The NQT had great problems controlling the pupils and very little help.
Involves regular teaching of the same class(es).	Yes, but the NQT taught 16 different classes per week and did not get the reduced timetable until halfway through the year.
Involves similar planning, teaching and assessment processes to those in which teachers working in substantive posts in the school are engaged.	Had no head of department for the spring and summer terms and little help from her in the autumn term. The only other teacher in the department was part-time, so the NQT had to support supply teachers.
Does not involve additional non-teaching responsibilities without the provision of appropriate preparation and support.	The NQT was a form tutor, but had no support.

Table 9.2   One NQT's job compared to what the induction circular lays down

These are the features of jobs that would be considered appropriate or 'reasonable' for a NQT.

1. *The post does not demand teaching outside the age range and subject(s) for which the NQT has been trained*

Examples of contraventions of this include:

●   a Maths teacher who has to teach PE without even the most basic of training in safety;

- a History teacher who has to teach Geography and RE to GCSE, even though he doesn't have such qualifications himself;
- a KS1- and KS2-trained teacher asked to teach reception.

2. *The post does not present the NQT on a day-to-day basis with acute or especially demanding discipline problems*

In an ideal world NQTs will be given timetables and classes that are comparatively easy. However, the easiest schools to work in often have the lowest staff turnover, so NQTs are rarely employed in them. More typically, NQTs will find themselves working in a tough school where there are 'especially demanding discipline problems'. Often NQTs, because they are appointed after everyone else has put in their bid for their class or timetable, will end up with a rough deal even in comparison to experienced members of staff.

3. *The post involves regular teaching of the same class or classes*

This isn't usually an issue for NQTs, but can be one for those who have entered a school as a supply or part-time teacher. During induction, you need to have a settled timetable, teaching the same pupils. If you are employed to work with pupils with special needs, or EAL, you should not be expected to cover classes for absent colleagues or teach other pupils, unless by prior consent and for a good educational reason.

4. *The post involves planning, teaching and assessment processes similar to those in which teachers working in substantive posts in the school are engaged*

Realistically, this should be interpreted as not being expected to keep meticulous planning and assessment files like you did on teaching practice. Since, however, you are responsible for demonstrating that you meet the standards for the end of the induction period, you may need and want to keep more detailed paperwork than a colleague, who perhaps appears to do very little written planning, and yet gets by.

An NQT had exactly the same number of pupils as the parallel class teacher who had 20 years' experience. A new girl arrived at the school. One would have thought that she would go into the experienced teacher's class, but actually she joined the NQT. The situation was made more difficult because the new girl couldn't read and hadn't been to school much before. This clearly made the NQT's planning, teaching and assessment harder than her colleague's.

5. *The post does not involve additional non-teaching responsibilities without the provision of appropriate preparation and support*

Additional non-teaching responsibilities can cover a range of things such as taking clubs, doing dinner duties and having management responsibility. This clause is there to protect you – from yourself as much as from others. New teachers are typically terribly keen and enthusiastic and want to set up clubs and innovate in the teaching of a curriculum area. However, all these things are extremely demanding and can distract you from what should be your main focus: your everyday teaching. Once you have got that tapped (if that ever happens!) you can develop further in other areas.

> Since my HoD and mentor has been suspended from school I have been running a one-man show. I have been setting cover work, sorting out discipline problems for supply teachers and organising many things that are beyond my job description.

If you find yourself taking an additional non-teaching responsibility you should have 'appropriate preparation and support'. This should start with an acknowledgement of the fact that you should not have to do this (refer to the induction guidance) but will do so if given support. What would be helpful? Shadowing someone or sharing their tutor group, being given some training in the pastoral aspect of teaching or receiving help with managing parents would be valuable. If you find yourself a subject leader, you should have a clear picture about what is expected of you, and given training and time to perform the role.

The induction tutor

The induction tutor has the day-to-day responsibility for your monitoring, support and assessment. They should be appropriately experienced and have regular contact with you. In many primary schools the induction tutor will be the deputy headteacher or a phase coordinator. In a secondary school there are normally at least two levels of support – the HoD and a senior member of staff. Schools organise induction personnel in a range of ways, such as:

Primary school 1 (mono-support)

Induction tutor:	Member of the senior management team (SMT)

Primary school 2 (mono-support)

Induction tutor:	Headteacher

Primary school 3 (bi-support)

Induction tutor:	Member of the SMT
Mentor:	Parallel class teacher

Primary school 4 (tri-support)

Induction coordinator:	Member of the SMT
Induction tutor:	Year group leader
Buddy mentor:	Recently qualified teacher

Secondary school 1 (mono-support)

Induction tutor:	Senior member of staff

Secondary school 2 (bi-support)

Induction coordinator:	Senior member of staff in charge of all NQTs in the school
Induction tutor:	HoD

Secondary school 3 (tri-support)

Induction coordinator:	Senior member of staff in charge of all NQTs in the school
Induction tutor:	HoD

| Buddy mentor: | Recently qualified teacher |

Secondary school 4 (tri-support)

Induction tutor/ coordinator:	Senior teacher who organises the induction programme, meetings, assessment reports, etc.
Academic mentor:	HoD who advises on all subject-related matters
Pastoral mentor:	Head of year who gives guidance on behaviour management and pastoral issues

Secondary school 5 (multi-support)

Staff Development Officer:	In charge of coordinating the induction programme for all NQTs and organises contracts, job descriptions, staff handbook and the pre-induction visits before the NQTs start work
Subject mentor:	Head of the department that the NQT works in; supervises planning and teaching and gives subject-specific input
Pastoral mentor:	Head of year who gives guidance on behaviour management and pastoral issues
Buddy mentor group:	Group of recently qualified teachers who provide a shoulder to cry on.

The terms by which roles are known varies.

One might imagine that the more people an NQT gets support from the better, and indeed we found instances where people benefited from getting help from a range of colleagues. However, some NQTs suffer as a result of responsibility being shared. For instance, an NQT in a secondary school with two levels of support suffered because the HoD did not do their job properly (observing every half term, setting and reviewing targets and having regular meetings). It was only at the end of term that the induction coordinator realised this, however.

On the other hand, sharing responsibility means that the induction tutor's considerable workload is lessened. Shared responsibility worked best in schools with good communication systems.

Responsibilities

Induction tutors are responsible for the following.

1. Making sure that you know and understand the roles and responsibilities of those involved in induction, including your own rights and your responsibility to take an active role in your professional development. Where NQTs are well supported, the induction tutor is up-to-date on induction requirements, has read the key documentation and is able to transmit this information to you and all others involved. Many schools now have an induction policy that gives clear guidance, particularly on everyone's rights and responsibilities.

2. Organising and implementing, in consultation with you, a tailored programme of monitoring, support and assessment that takes forward in a flexible way the action plan for your professional development and which takes into account the needs and strengths identified at the end of training, the core standards, and the specific context of the school.

3. Coordinating or carrying out observations of your teaching and organising follow-up discussions. You should be observed at least once every half term, and the first observation should take place within the first four weeks of starting teaching. You should also have a post-observation discussion about your teaching. If different people are carrying out observations, they need to be coordinated so that you are not given conflicting messages.

4. Reviewing your progress against your objectives and the standards. Progress should be reviewed every half term and summarised officially in the assessment forms at the end of each term. It's in everyone's interests therefore that objectives are SMART (specific, measurable, achievable, realistic and time-bound). I would also add that they should be clearly understandable, particularly in terms of the success criteria.

5. Making sure that you are fully informed about the nature and

purpose of assessment in the induction period. One NQT who failed to complete his induction period satisfactorily complained that he did not always know when things were being said to him 'officially', that is as part of the assessment process, and when people were offering advice supportively. It's essential that you are clear about the status of advice and comments, particularly since the monitoring, support and assessment may be carried out by the same person. It's difficult and uncomfortable for them as well as for you.

6. Ensuring that dated records are kept of monitoring and support, and of formative and summative assessment activities undertaken, and their outcomes. There are examples of what these might look like in this book and in my *Successful Induction for New Teachers* (Bubb, 2007).

The induction tutor needs to be fully aware of the requirements of the induction period and to have the skills, expertise and knowledge needed to work effectively in the role. This has been an issue for many NQTs. Too frequently, induction tutors have not been fully aware of what the induction period is all about. Many have been surprised that they are no longer simply mentors, there to help if the need arises. Their 'skills, knowledge and expertise' vary. Indeed, there is no definition of what is 'good enough' in this respect. Some have attended induction tutor training to help them in their role, but many have not. Some have read the key documentation and others have not. In particular, they should be able to provide or coordinate effective guidance and support, and to make rigorous and fair judgements about the new teacher's performance in relation to the core standards. Quite a tall order!

If you have problems with your induction tutor or any other people who are responsible for your induction, you must be proactive in trying to resolve them. It's you and the pupils you teach who will suffer. Here are some issues or problems relating to induction tutors that NQTs have encountered, based on my research:

- hasn't time to do the job;
- doesn't want to do the job;
- not experienced in the NQT's subject or age group;

- doesn't know what to do;
- not planning how the induction release time should be spent – leaving it up to the new teacher;
- not observing;
- observing too often;
- personality clash;
- different educational philosophy;
- NQT doesn't value what induction tutor has to say.

When one asks NQTs what they value most about their induction tutors they are very clear:

1. They were always available for advice.
2. They gave me a regular meeting time, even though they were busy.
3. They were genuinely interested in how I was doing.
4. They were honest and open, which encouraged trust.
5. They listened to me – and didn't impose their own views.
6. They made practical suggestions.
7. They shared their expertise, ideas and resources.
8. They were encouraging and optimistic – they made me feel good.
9. They stopped me working myself into the ground by setting realistic objectives.
10. They weren't perfect themselves, which was reassuring!
11. They looked after me, keeping parents and the head off my back.
12. Their feedback after observations was useful. Good to get some praise and ideas for improvements.
13. It helped when they wrote the end of term reports because these gave us a clear picture of how we were doing.
14. They were well organised, and if they said they'd do something they did it.

More than anything, NQTs value someone who gives them time. This is a very precious resource in schools. Induction tutors often have many other time-consuming roles and their time spent on induction is rarely funded. The government has rightly devoted money to ensuring that NQTs have a 10 per cent reduced timetable, but there is little extra to cover the potentially enormous costs of paying the people who are doing the support, monitoring and assessment. Many take on the role thinking that it's just a support-ive one, whereas actually it takes up a lot of time and calls for a great deal of skill. The end-of-term report takes about two hours to write; meetings take at least 30 minutes per week; observations take half a day every half term if you count the preparation and feedback time too. So the job significantly adds to workload. As ever, much has to be done on goodwill. Headteachers need to realise this and reduce their teaching load accordingly.

The next chapter will help you to make the most of induction such, as by seizing opportunities for professional development based on an accurate identification of your priorities and setting objectives to help you make rapid progress.

ten

Making the most of induction

- Professional portfolio
- Setting objectives
- The individualised induction programme
- Observing others
- Being observed
- Half-termly reviews
- Being assessed

Induction exists to help new teachers. Don't see it as a threat or a hurdle, but as a great opportunity to make rapid progress in a short amount of time. This chapter offers advice on portfolios, induction programmes and the assessment procedures.

Professional portfolio

Induction leads from training for QTS into early and continuing professional development (CPD), ideally in a fairly seamless manner. So, it seems to me that a portfolio or folder that spans this career-long period is beneficial. It will be the repository of all CV material, a place to record all your professional development and a way to reflect on this, in order to plan more. It is a way of using past experiences and present activities to demonstrate and reflect on skills learnt, to identify future learning needs and priorities and to inform and plan prospective development.

Specifically, the professional portfolio will help you to:

- gather evidence for
  - induction
  - promotion and job interviews
  - performance review meetings.
- plan your career by
  - recording your career history and professional development
  - collecting evidence of achievements
  - showing skills and/or improvement in areas such as team building, working together, motivating people, self-confidence, etc.
  - reflecting on your progress as a teacher.
- plan your training and development by
  - reflecting on your teaching and learning
  - analysing strengths
  - identifying and targeting learning and development opportunities
  - planning for qualifications.

It should not be onerous to keep. The induction guidance says:

> Under normal circumstances, your work as a teacher and ongoing professional dialogue as part of your monitoring and support programme will provide evidence in relation to meeting the standards. You will not be expected to maintain an additional evidence base.

Here's how you could organise the contents.

The professional portfolio

1. Career history

a. CV and qualifications
b. references
c. job descriptions.

2. Training

a. Monitoring of teaching (e.g. observations)
b. action plans for objectives.

3. *Induction year*

a. Evidence of effectiveness at Professional Review Meeting (at half term)
b. monitoring of teaching (e.g. at least six observations)
c. assessment forms (three when on induction)
d. professional development activities and meetings, e.g. handouts and certificates from courses attended; notes from observing other staff; articles read and websites visited; list of networks made.

4. *Other information*

a. Policies for induction, CPD and performance management (PM)
b. information about advanced skills and lead teachers.

Setting objectives

You should be setting objectives for what you want to do better – and to get you where you want to go. Your main concern is to be a good class teacher and meet the standards. But you may have a further ambition that you want to work towards. Setting yourself a goal, a target, an objective (don't get bogged down in the semantics) will provide you with a framework for doing a complex job at a very fast pace. Objectives encourage you to prioritise and give you a sense of achievement when they are met.

Don't stick slavishly to what you wrote at the end of your training course. The chances are that your new job makes much of this irrelevant. You might have been very good at managing behaviour on teaching practice but now have the class from hell. Think about what's going to really help you now – and what will make you a better teacher of your pupils. Your induction tutor will help you prioritise and pace yourself. It's good to set one objective as a result of an observation of your teaching. Remember that your aim is to meet the standards and to help your pupils learn.

Some new teachers have plenty of discussion about what they need to improve, but no specific objectives. This is a missed opportunity. The very act of writing objectives down clarifies what you need to do, and helps ensure that they're SMART. Ask yourself if the objective is specific, measurable, achievable, relevant and time-bound – and adapt it to make sure it is. An objective like 'improve control' is too large, and could be a lifetime's work. It's better to be more specific about what needs most urgent attention, such as: 'By the end of term improve control particularly after breaktimes, during independent activities and when tidying up.' This is achievable and relevant to your class teaching.

Aim for an objective to be met within half a term, to give you a sense of achievement. That's how often reviews with your induction tutor take place. Fairly short-term goals will encourage

Objective: To develop classroom management skills in order to improve behaviour and lesson timings.		
Success criteria	Actions	When by
Lessons will adhere to set times with the majority of work completed as set	• Review planning to look at why lessons might be over-running (with a focus on carpet time and moving around the classroom)	1 October
	• Talk through planning with Key Stage Coordinator/Mentor	4 October
	• Plan for simpler activities in the short term, while children adapt to new ways of working – expectations	8 October
	• Keep clock in prominent place and keep checking the time	10 October
	• Use a timer for different sections of the lesson	10 October
Fewer incidences of children being moved to Red on the traffic lights	• Recap school rules with the class	2 October
	• Continue using traffic lights according to school policy	10 October
	• Observe Mentor teaching own class for use of behaviour management strategies	5 October
	• Trial strategies in class and develop list of those that work for you	24 October
	• Praise children for their improved behaviour	17 October
	• Consider sending mini-certificates home	17 October
Plan for effective classroom organisation	• Plan simplified activities	2 October
	• Establish routines and expectations	4 October
	• Build in opportunities to develop independence	17 October

Figure 10.1   An action plan to meet an objective

you to be realistic and stay focused. When you're happy with the objective, break it down into bite-sized chunks – steps or success criteria – and think what you'll have to do and what help you'll need. Write this action plan in the easiest way. Figure 10.1 is a useful format for a working document.

The individualised induction programme

The vast majority of teachers feel under tremendous pressure in their first year of teaching. The individualised induction programme, however, is the key to your successful progress, and sanity. You have release time and rights that previous cohorts of new teachers have not had. You need to make the most of them – you'll never have the opportunity again.

Planning an effective programme, however, isn't easy. There are many components, as we shall see. There is no such thing as a perfect model because every context and every teacher is different. Even in the same school, what works for one person may not work for another. The statutory guidance emphasises that induction programmes should be 'tailored to individual needs'. Your induction tutor is responsible for drawing up the programme, but you need to play a big part to ensure it meets your needs.

A significant feature of the statutory induction programmes is that they should involve 'a combination of support, monitoring and assessment'. In the past, support has been the focus of most programmes. Monitoring and assessment have been very much in the background. There should be a balance between support, monitoring and assessment, and you should alert people if you feel that one is dominating to the detriment of others.

The induction programme should have specific weekly events, involving support, monitoring and assessment. The filling in of a diary sheet such as Figure 10.2 will help you plan and briefly record specifics with your induction tutor. It can be used for evaluating the programme, and as a record to show the LA and other external monitors. It shows how all the elements can be brought together in a manageable way, and how the programme can respond to the NQT's stages of development and half-termly objectives through the year.

Objective: To improve procedures for assessment to inform planning, by 20 February

Observed on	Things to do in 10 per cent reduced timetable	Induction tutor meeting focus	School inset
6 January	Review last term's progress	Plan half-term meetings and activities	Thinking skills
13 January	Get a detailed picture of what three pupils can do Set targets	Assessment coordinator – target setting	Thinking skills
20 January	23 January course on assessment	24 January induction tutor training	Target setting
27 January	Observation focusing on assessment in lesson	Assessment coordinator – monitoring targets	Charity week
3 February Observation focusing on assessment	Look at marking and record keeping of two other teachers	Discuss observation Prepare for parents' evening	Numeracy
10 February	Observation focusing on assessment in lesson	Review progress	Parents' evening

Figure 10.2   An induction programme

The school–based programme has several elements that need to be seen as a whole in contributing to your development:

- school/phase/departmental staff meetings;
- meetings with the induction tutor;
- how to spend your reduced timetable;
- observation of your teaching.

School staff meetings and training will have an impact on your progress and so should be noted on your induction programme. There should be regular, planned meetings with the induction tutor. These should happen throughout the year. It's very easy to let them slide because of other demands on time, but you really will benefit from attention, particularly because of the formal assessment at the end of each term. Often, successful NQTs are left to their own devices, but they too need to be challenged in order to become even better teachers. One said: 'I think I was neglected because everyone was happy with me. But now I feel disappointed in myself because I know I should be doing better than I am.'

How often should induction meetings take place?

The answer to this question will depend on how much support you are getting from others. For instance, year-group planning and assessment meetings will be of enormous benefit. Similarly, making friends with someone on the staff with whom you can discuss issues will ease the burden on the induction tutor – as long as advice from different quarters isn't contradictory. Generally, I would recommend weekly meetings at first, maybe reducing to fortnightly after the first term. The induction guidance, however, implies a minimum of a meeting at the beginning and end of each half term.

Meetings should consist of quality time. Chats in the staff room at playtime may be pleasant, but cannot take the place of planned meetings. A regular meeting slot of about half an hour will be seen as the appropriate time to raise matters. Quality-time induction meetings should have:

- no interruptions;
- a venue without disturbance from phone calls, pupils, other teachers, etc.;
- a fixed start and finish time;
- an agreed agenda, albeit informal and flexible;
- an agreed aim, probably linked to the standards;
- a focus on the NQT, rather than the induction tutor's anecdotes;
- a record of any agreed outcomes.

How to spend your reduced timetable

How are you spending this release time? Any teacher will tell you it's a very precious resource, so make the most of it. It's all too easy to spend your induction time doing things that are immediately necessary – marking, say, or displays – but it's not always a good use of time in the long run. There are many different ways to spend induction release time:

1. reflecting on progress so far;
2. attending induction and other courses;
3. observing other teachers in the school;
4. observing teachers in other schools;
5. observing someone teach your class(es);
6. observing someone teach a lesson that you have planned;
7. observing how pupils of different ages learn;
8. looking at resources in the school;
9. visiting local education centres, museums and venues for outings;
10. arranging a school outing;
11. looking at the educational possibilities of the local environment;
12. working with the SENCO on writing individual education plans (IEPs);
13. reading pupils' previous records and reports;
14. improving subject knowledge through reading, observation, discussion;
15. analysing planning systems in order to improve your own;
16. analysing marking and record-keeping systems in order to improve your own;
17. learning more about strategies for teaching pupils with special needs and EAL;
18. learning more about strategies for teaching very able pupils;
19. preparing for parents' evenings;
20. meeting with outside agencies (e.g. social workers, educational psychologists);
21. discussing lesson observations;
22. meeting with the induction tutor and other staff.

When considering what to do, ask yourself whether it will help you meet the standards for the end of the induction year and whether you are going to be a better teacher as a result. If you make specific plans, you're less likely to lose your release time. Link activities to the objectives you're setting with your induction tutor. If marking takes hours, set yourself an objective to improve it. Spend some time reading articles on the subject and getting other people's tips for how they do it more quickly than you. Looking at their systems and what they write is really useful.

Spend time with other staff, like the SENCO or the gifted and talented lead teacher. Find out how best to teach certain groups of children. Talk through specific problems with them, as well as with your induction tutor. If you're in the secondary sector, it's fascinating to track a pupil for half a day and see what their experience of school is. You learn lots from seeing the styles of different subject teachers, and you gain an insight into how students learn. Certainly, helping pupils to make connections between subjects can really help to improve their work. Reading books and articles and finding ways to make your assessment systems more effective are all useful ways to spend time. Look through resources in the school – hunt around and you could find something fantastic by accident!

An important decision that needs to be made early on is whether you should join a programme with other NQTs. These courses are often run by local authorities, colleges and educational consultants. The big advantage of joining such a programme is that you gain a great deal from talking to other NQTs. You'll feel enormously comforted by hearing that others are going through the same problems. No matter how sympathetic experienced members of staff are, the solitary NQT in a school often feels that they are the only one who cannot, for instance, get their class to assembly on time. Enrolment on an externally organised programme also eases the burden on schools to provide training. However, it can only supplement the individualised school programme, not replace it. Check that any course will be covering what you need to improve. Don't just look at ones run locally – cast your net wider to find just the right one. Remember that you're being inducted into the profession, not just your school. Keep your ears open to everything, but keep thinking about how you could use ideas in your classroom.

You may benefit from finding out more about outside agencies, particularly if any of your pupils are seen by them. You could sit in on some of the work of educational psychologists, health visitors, educational welfare officers, speech therapist or occupational therapists. Go to different sorts of educational settings. If your school has a link with a special school or pupil referral unit, make an appointment to visit them and look around. Get to know the local area around the school, look at where the children live and the places they talk about. Some could have educational possibilities but, even if they don't, the experience will give you some insight into the children's lives and help you keep up with breaktime conversations.

It's a good idea to plan a class visit while you have the safety net of still being a new teacher. It takes lots of organisation and even choosing a good venue can take ages. You need to visit it beforehand and do a risk assessment of all points on the journey and at the venue. This will give you the chance to think through potential problems and avoid things that could go wrong.

Reflection time is a must. It should have higher status and time allocated to it. Analyse why things go well, and why other things don't go so well. Most of all, make sure you spend the time becoming a better teacher.

Another problem with the release time is what happens to your class when you are not there. Some NQTs preferred not to take their 10 per cent release time because of the disruption to the class caused by different supply teachers. They found that they would have to teach lessons again because the pupils had not learned things with the supply teacher. This is a particular problem for new teachers in Scotland, with 30 per cent of their timetable being covered by a relief teacher. It's very important to have school staff covering the induction release time. Classes can go haywire when they have a supply teacher. One school, which had four NQTs, employed a further NQT on a one-year contract so that an experienced member of staff could be non-class based and so cover all the NQTs' release time.

Observing others

An excellent way of spending your release time is to observe others at work. You'll find out so much about teaching and learning. Over the year, observe a range of teachers and other staff, age groups, specialist groups, subjects and lessons at different times of the day. Keep a record of observations and note down what you learned – and what you did differently as a result. Observe in other schools, too. You'll learn a great deal from seeing other NQTs. It's cheering to see that everyone has similar problems and it's fascinating to study the different ways people manage them. If you watch your class being taught by someone else, you can see the children's learning, behaviour and reactions, and how another teacher handles them.

Lesson observations of other teachers have great value for NQTs' development as effective teachers. One induction tutor said: 'The NQTs have probably observed more staff this year than some people who have been here for six or seven years.' My research found that most respondents conducted only between three and five observations of other teacher. However, it seems a disappointingly small number, considering the NQTs' opportunity to benefit from such a valuable resource.

You need to have a focus for your observation. There is so much to see that you can end up getting overwhelmed. First, decide what you want to observe. Ideally, link the observation to one of your objectives – something that you want to develop. For instance, if you want to improve pace in introductions, arrange to observe that. Notice the speed of the exposition, how many pupils answer questions and how the teacher manages to move them on, how instructions are given, resources distributed, and how off-task behaviour is dealt with. Here are some examples of how some NQTs chose what to observe.

Julian was interested in developing his explanations of mathematical concepts so that he could make things clearer and not get thrown by pupils' questions. With this clearly in mind, he chose to observe Maths lessons where new topics were being started. He learned the benefits of rock-solid subject knowledge and scaffolding information. He also gained a broader repertoire of questioning techniques that he was able to try out in his own teaching.

Diana had problems with behaviour management, so observed a teacher with a good reputation for control. She gained some ideas, but found that much of this experienced teacher's control was 'invisible' – he just cleared his throat and the class became quiet. So, she observed a supply teacher, and someone with only a little more experience than herself. It was hard to persuade them to let her observe, but when they realised how fruitful the experience and the discussions afterwards would be, they accepted. These lessons, though not so perfectly controlled, gave Diana much more to think about and she learned lots of useful strategies. Both teachers found it useful to have Diana's views on the lesson, as a non-threatening observer, so they too gained from the experience.

Miranda's objective was to share learning intentions with pupils, so she observed a teacher who was known to be good at this. She not only listened well to the teacher's explanation of what he wanted the pupils to achieve, but saw that he wrote different lesson outcomes for each group under the heading 'What I'm looking for'. As well as focusing on the teacher, she watched the pupils carefully and spoke to them about their understanding of what they were doing and why. This gave her insight into children's learning and areas of confusion.

Once you've decided what you would like to observe you need to arrange it. It's useful for your induction tutor to be involved in the arrangements, particularly for observations in another school. Their involvement will lend weight to your request and increase the chances of it happening.

You need to discuss the observation with the teacher. Remember that they are doing you a favour and that they'll probably be apprehensive about you being in the classroom so you will need to be sensitive. Be clear about what you would like to see, and why. You will need to arrange a mutually convenient time. This isn't always easy because of timetabling constraints.

When you're observing

If possible read the lesson plan, paying particular attention to the learning objective. Is it a useful objective, and is it shared with the pupils? Choose somewhere to sit which is outside the direct line of the teacher's vision, but where you can see the pupils and what the teacher is doing. When the pupils are doing activities, move around to ascertain the effectiveness of the explanation, organisation and choice of task. Look at different groups (girls and boys; high, average and low attainers; and pupils with EAL) to see whether everyone's needs are being met.

Think about the pupils' learning and what it is about the teaching that is helping or hindering it. Try to note cause and effect.

For instance, what was it about the teacher's delivery that caused pupils' rapt attention or made them fidget? Note what pupils actually achieve. Teachers are not always aware that some pupils have only managed to write the date and that others have exceeded expectations. Look through pupils' books to get a feel. Avoid teaching the pupils yourself or interfering in any way. This is very tempting! For example, pupils will often expect you to help them with spellings, but once you help one, others will ask for help too.

Think about the teaching and learning you have seen and try to talk about it with the teacher. Note down a few key things you have seen, using Figure 10.3 or one of the observation sheets from Chapter 4. Is there anything that could impact on your teaching?

Teacher:	Year group:	Date and time:
Ideas		What and when implemented
Arrangement of the room		
Resources		
Behaviour management		
Teaching strategies		

Figure 10.3 Observing other teachers: what have you learned?

The Insider's Guide for New Teachers, Routledge © Sara Bubb 2010

It's even worthwhile to observe teaching that you do not like because it makes you think about your own practice, and almost forces you to articulate your educational philosophy – something we do too little of.

Being observed

You'll be observed at least once every half term when you're an NQT, and often more. In the national induction research (Totterdell *et al.*, 2002) I was surprised to find that 89 per cent of NQTs found it really useful. I had thought that people would have been sick of being observed during their training, and see more observations as an unnecessary stress. The views of this NQT were typical: 'It's vital. It's just so informative having someone watch you teach because you can't see everything and sometimes you don't see what you do well, as well as the things you need to develop.'

It's considered the most nerve wracking part but I think it's the most effective. Many spoke of it as a positive and constructive experience. One NQT loved being observed: 'I love showing my kids off as well ... I choose my lowest sets .... It raises their self esteem and it makes me feel really proud of them.'

However, not all schools are as organised about carrying out observations as they should be because:

- there were too many other things to do at the beginning of the school year;
- induction tutors thought that NQTs needed time to settle before being observed – this was often misplaced kindness;
- induction tutors didn't know that they should do an early observation and hadn't been trained to do so.

Be proactive in asking for the date of observations. Some NQTs have had observations that took place on the last day of term, with no notice. A variety of people can observe NQTs teach: induction tutors, headteachers, mentors, heads of department and representatives from the AB's advisers or inspectors.

Try to see observation of your teaching as an opportunity to get some really useful feedback – and not as a threat. Observation is a powerful tool for assessing and monitoring your progress. Used well, it can be a way to support you, because observation gives such a detailed picture and enables very specific objectives to be set. The value of observation, however, depends on how well it's planned, executed and discussed afterwards. It's almost always a stressful experience: protocols help.

Before an observation

Make sure you know what notice you'll have of an observation, when you're going to be observed, for how long and by whom. Discuss nitty gritty things such as exactly when they'll arrive and leave, where they will sit, how their presence is to be explained to the pupils and how they should be introduced. Find out what format the observer is going to write in (an example is in Figure 10.4) and when you'll be able to get feedback on the lesson. This does not need to be graded, although some schools use the Ofsted lesson criteria: just in case you're judged on this, have a look at Table 10.1.

It's useful to have a focus for the observation – something that is being looked at in particular. This won't stop the observer from noticing and commenting on other things, but will ensure that you have information on the key area that you are working on. Think about what will really help you. Here are examples of what some people choose as a focus.

- Feedback (oral and written):
  - How well do different groups know what they are doing?
  - How well do different groups know why they are doing it?
  - How do different groups know how well they have done?
  - What sort of feedback does the teacher use, and to which children?
- Learning objectives:
  - How well are these conveyed?
  - Are they appropriate for different groups of children?
  - Do the activities enable them to achieve the objectives?
  - Do all children meet them well enough?
- Management:
  - Is there good control at different parts of the lesson and of all the children?

Summary of classroom observation

Strengths of the lesson
Well done, Juliet, this was a lesson that I enjoyed. You have so many talents as a teacher! In particular the strengths of this lesson were:
- Your clear enjoyment of teaching and self confidence
- Strong voice, good intonation – clear explanations
- Warmth towards the students – your smile, eye contact, facial expressions and body language all work to encourage and give students the confidence to take risks. V. positive feedback and use of praise to boost self confidence
- Good questioning esp. stretching EAL pupils to explain what they mean
- Excellent control – all the above contribute help in this area but you are also very confident yourself and this helps. You expect them to behave in a certain way, and they do. You handle the odd misbehaviour briskly with a change of tone ('don't call out, Michael') and good use of body language (turning away, not giving attention) but then you catch M being good – brilliant!
- Well resourced and organised. Clear plan, with timings. Good use made of the whiteboard
- Good use of support teacher at start of lesson and in reading out a paragraph to emphasise the tense difference. Good choice of text that motivates and is part of their culture

Areas for further development
1. Try to increase the learning of more of the students more of the time, e.g.:
- Share learning objective; big picture of the lesson
- More paired work
- Having a plenary for them and you to evaluate learning and progress
- Make even more use of support teacher

Teacher's comment
Thank you. This has been very helpful and has boosted my confidence while giving me clear direction.

Figure 10.4   Summary of classroom observation

- How is off-task behaviour managed?
- Is there a brisk pace that keeps children's attention?
- Are resources appropriate, organised and distributed to make best use of time?

Being nervous when observed is perfectly normal, and most people can tell when you are and make allowances for this. Chapter 4 has some ideas for how to prepare for an observation. Give the observer a copy of your plan so that they are clear why you are doing certain things, but otherwise just block out the observer and focus on teaching and learning. Be flexible where necessary but

Description	Characteristics of the lesson
Outstanding (1)	The lesson is at least good in all major respects and is exemplary in significant elements, as shown by the significant progress made by all of the learners.
Good (2)	Most learners make good progress because of the good teaching they receive. Behaviour overall is good and learners are well motivated. They work in a safe, secure and friendly environment. Teaching is based on secure subject knowledge with a well-structured range of stimulating tasks that engage the learners. The work is well matched to the full range of learners' needs, so that most are suitably challenged. Teaching methods are effectively related to the lesson objectives and the needs of learners. Teaching assistants and resources are well deployed and good use is made of time. Assessment of learners' work is regular, consistent and promotes progress.
Satisfactory (3)	The lesson is inadequate in no major respect, and may be good in some respects, as shown by the satisfactory enjoyment and progress of the learners.

Inadequate (4)	A lesson cannot be adequate if:
	• most learners, or a significant specific minority of learners, make less than satisfactory progress;
	• learners' overall behaviour or attitudes are unsatisfactory, spiritual, moral, social and cultural development are neglected, and learners' overall personal development is poor;
	• the health or safety of the learners is endangered;
	• the teaching is unsatisfactory. Unsatisfactory teaching is likely to have one or more of the following:
	  – weak knowledge of the curriculum leading to inaccurate teaching and low demands on pupils;
	  – work badly matched to the pupils' starting points;
	  – ineffective classroom management of behaviour;
	  – methods which are poorly geared to the learning objectives or which fail to gain the interest and commitment of the learners;
	  – inadequate use of resources, including assistants and the time available;
	  – poor assessment.

Guidance on where to pitch judgements about the overall quality of a lesson:
The overall judgement will be a 'best fit' of the grade descriptions in the box, except in the case of an unsatisfactory lesson where particular conditions mean that the lesson cannot be satisfactory.

Table 10.1 Ofsted's lesson grading

don't forget to reinforce and assess learning. Try to demonstrate the standards.

Don't panic if things start to go wrong. Think on your feet. Most NQTs have some lessons that go swimmingly, others that are okay and occasional disasters. You can learn from all of them. There are a huge number of factors to do with you and what you're teaching and then a whole heap to do with different classes, what lesson they've just had and what time of day it is.

The post-observation discussion

The value of the dialogue that takes place when feedback is given after a lesson observation cannot be over-emphasised. Reflecting on your own teaching through discussing a lesson observation may be your most valuable learning experience. Its effect, however, depends on both the quality of the feedback and the relationship of trust between you and the observer.

After the lesson, think about what the pupils learned and why, so that you're ready to answer the inevitable 'How do you think it went?' question. Before discussing the lesson, reflect on it yourself. What were you pleased with? What could have gone better? How did your teaching affect the progress pupils made? Don't be disheartened if the lesson didn't go well. See it as an event to be learnt from and given advice on. There's no such thing as a perfect teacher (except in your mind), so your lesson doesn't have to be perfect. You need to show that you're reflective, making progress and acting on advice. However, if you think your teaching is criticised unfairly, make sure you explain the reasoning behind your actions. Ask for advice and ideas. Afterwards, reflect on the discussion. Feel good about the positive comments and think about how to improve.

Half-termly reviews

Your progress should be reviewed half-termly using a proforma, such as Figure 10.5. Take stock and appreciate what you've learned and how far you've come on your journey to being the best teacher in the world. Maybe you've had to go off course from the way you want to teach for all manner of pragmatic reasons –

Date and time
Things that are going well
Things to improve
How is induction going?
Signatures

Figure 10.5 Professional review meeting

say, the kids behave better in rows but that's not how you want to work in the long term. Look at your induction entitlement. Did you get it all last term? If not, you need to make sure it happens in the future. Alternatively, people may have provided good support in the first term, but then forget that you're still an NQT (you're so good!) and need help throughout the year.

Be clear about what support you want. Have you got a clear picture of how well you're doing? The end-of-term assessment report should have detailed this. If the headteacher and induction tutor have decided that you're not making satisfactory progress you should get extra support and monitoring from the school and LA to enable you to pass the induction standards by the end of the year. Most of you will be making satisfactory or better progress. You'll always be thinking about what's going to help you be a better class teacher. Don't get distracted from this most complex and important journey. Running clubs and taking other roles in the school can be an unnecessary and lengthy diversion.

Being assessed

Many NQTs worry about what they must do to pass induction. Don't panic. If you've been teaching for a year you will have been doing all that is necessary to meet the standards. Get them out and assess yourself against them. You will have been setting targets, planning, teaching, assessing, managing pupils, using IEPs, working with support staff, talking to parents, implementing school policies and taking an active part in your professional development. You don't need to collect any evidence for the standards other than what you do as part of your job, and what others have written about you. However, look through the standards to check you haven't left any gaps.

Some schools expect NQTs to keep teaching practice-level folders of evidence, but this is unnecessary. You keep enough paperwork as a class teacher. Don't worry about standards that don't apply to you – if you don't teach pupils with special needs, you can't contribute to IEPs.

The three formal assessment meetings are very important, and valuable, in reviewing progress. They should be held towards the end of each term, and are the forum for the termly assessment reports to be discussed and written. Schools are obviously busy at the end of term, so put a date in the diary for your assessment meetings with the headteacher and induction tutor. Choose a date that is convenient to all and make sure that at least one week's notice is given. It is ideal if it takes place during the school day, though in practice I'm sure that many schools will find this hard to organise. Think carefully about a realistic start and finish time – it will be important to feel fresh. The length of the meeting will depend on the degree of agreement about your performance and how much preparatory work on the report has been done. A straightforward case for which all are well briefed should take not much more than half an hour. Holding the meeting in your class-room may give you a feeling of control that may not be present in the headteacher's office. It also means that there is easy access to further evidence, such as pupils' work.

Standardised three-page forms have to be filled in and sent to the AB within ten days of the meeting. ABs will usually set their own deadlines for reports. The form for the first and second terms requires the headteacher to tick one of two statements:

• The above named teacher's progress indicates that he/she is making satisfactory progress towards meeting the Core Standards for the satisfactory completion of the induction period.

- The above named teacher's progress indicates that he/she may not be able to meet the Core Standards for the satisfactory completion of the induction period.

You'll know if you're at risk of failure because observations of your teaching and the first and/or second term's reports would have said your progress was unsatisfactory. If they did not, you are unlikely to be anywhere near failing. The system does not allow for last-minute shocks. To be sure, check with your headteacher. If you aren't making satisfactory progress after the first or second term, the assessment report and meeting should mean that you're clear about what you have to do to improve.

The headteacher must also indicate that the NQT has 'experienced monitoring and support in line with the statutory guidance'. These are:

- observations of the NQT's teaching and the provision of feedback;
- discussions between the NQT and the induction tutor to review progress and set objectives;
- observations of experienced teachers by the NQT;
- an assessment meeting between the NQT and the induction tutor.

The induction tutor will probably be responsible for writing the reports. Make sure you are happy with what is written about you – that it is a fair reflection of you. During the assessment meeting, suggest additions or revisions to the wording of the assessment form.

NQTs can choose whether or not to make a comment on the report, and are given a box in which to write. I think you should write something since the whole emphasis in induction is on being proactive and reflective. Some NQTs say which parts of their induction programme have been most useful; others defend themselves; others write about what they feel are their strengths and areas for development. Here is one example:

> Having read the above report I feel that it is a clear description of my term so far. Whilst I got to know the children relatively

quickly, I am aware that there is still a need for me to develop my understanding of each individual child's needs; my focus for development must relate to enthusing and challenging the more able children in my class. The support I have received at this school has been of a high standard. A long talk with my mentor has highlighted the need for me to be more open with any problems, concerns or needs I may have.

Your headteacher has to say whether or not you're meeting the standards at the end of your third term. This becomes a recommendation that is sent to the LA as AB. The AB should have been involved with new teachers whose first and second term assessment reports indicated problems. They make the final decision and will send a list of those who have passed to the GTC. Those who fail are deregistered from the GTC and never again allowed to teach in a maintained school or non-maintained special school. Don't worry, only about 25 fail each year.

Those at risk of failing are often encouraged to leave before they have completed their third term. They can complete their last term on induction at another school and at another time. Often this fresh start can pay dividends, and it's the route I'd take if I were failing.

The last report should outline how well you're meeting the standards. Use the time to get a clear picture of your strengths and successes, and celebrate them. Discuss what you should develop in your second year when you get slotted into the school's PM arrangements. Sign the report, make a comment, take a photocopy and check (and keep checking) that it is received by the AB.

Case study: how Jill completed the assessment on William

Both Jill and William evaluated how they thought he was meeting the standards by jotting notes about each. They discussed their views, ensuring that evidence existed for all assertions. She drafted sections of the report against the three headings of the standards, aiming for a word length of 300 words. She wrote an overall message in the first sentence and then elaborated. Where space allowed, she referred briefly to evidence.

Jill gave a copy to the headteacher and William to look at just before the meeting. At the meeting, all discussed what was written and suggested changes. The revised, agreed document was then given to William for a written comment, and then he, Jill and the headteacher signed it. All were given copies and the original was sent to the LA.

Failing

If the school decides that you have not met the core standards the headteacher must detail:

- where the standards have been met;
- areas of weakness in standards that have not been met;
- the evidence used to inform the judgement.

In cases of either a successful or a failing NQT, the headteacher is only making a recommendation to the AB. It is up to them to make the final decision. In the case of failures, many ABs will want to observe the NQT, but this is not statutory. The AB is responsible for making sure that the assessment of the NQT was accurate and reliable, that the NQT's objectives were set appropriately and that they were supported. In exceptional circumstances, ABs can grant extensions to the induction period. These are where, for reasons beyond the control of one or more of the parties involved, it would be unreasonable to expect the NQT to have met the core standards. Such reasons might include:

- personal crises, illness, disability or other reasons relating to the NQT;
- issues around the support during induction;
- where there is insufficient evidence for a decision about whether the core standards have been met to be made.

NQTs can appeal to the GTC against the AB's decision to extend the induction period or fail them. The appeal procedures are set out in Section 5 of the induction guidance, but I'm sure you will not need them.

Scotland

The system of assessing new teachers in Scotland is different, although there are similarities. In their first year, new teachers, or 'probationers' as they are called, are given 'provisional registration'. By the end of the year they have to demonstrate that they meet the Standard for Full Registration. As in England, the school is responsible for the recommendation, although full registration is awarded by the GTCS. The school has to make one of the following recommendations:

- that full registration be granted; or
- that the period of provisional registration be extended; or
- that registration be withdrawn.

Do you notice that the school has the option of recommending an extension? This can't happen in England. In Scotland the Profile (the assessment form) is completed twice, rather than three times as in England. It is eight pages long and combines the Interim and Final Profile.

Problems

Well, that's what is meant to happen and for many people the process is straightforward and reassuring. Unfortunately, there are cases of poor practice. Perhaps you can learn from problems that some people have encountered – and try to avoid having similar things happen to you.

Problem 1

I had my assessment meeting today. It lasted 10 minutes during my lunch hour! The meeting was just between my induction tutor and me. I was given a copy of the report to read and given a form on which I can write my own comments. I hadn't quite imagined it to be like that.

This shouldn't happen. Lunchtime is not an ideal time for an assessment meeting. If the NQT is upset by something that has been written, this will have an effect on the afternoon's teaching. The absence of the headteacher (who should have been there), it lasting only ten minutes, it happening at lunchtime and the NQT not really having an opportunity to affect what was written at the meeting all give messages that the assessment and the NQT are not important.

Problem 2

> My school have just realised they have to send a report to the LA. I haven't had any support from my mentor all term (due to the headteacher delegating everything else to her) and have been struggling to meet my targets on my own. I've only had 2 weeks with release time this half-term so observation of other staff have gone by the wayside, as have observations of my teaching. There is not time for my review this term so it is being left until next! I just hope I pass.

I hope situations like this are rare. She could have raised the issue of lack of support and the 10 per cent reduced timetable earlier in the term, with the mentor and headteacher, and then the person in charge of NQTs at the LA. I would question why there wasn't time for her review. It sounds as if she has low status and the induction regulations have low priority. However, the school is breaking the law in not providing the induction entitlement and she and all the children who are ever going to be taught by her will suffer the consequences. I wouldn't be surprised if this person moved to a school that did value her. Illness should be the only reason why an assessment meeting and report are postponed. Being busy is a fact of life, highly predictable and so is not an excuse. The school is making itself very vulnerable. The boxes outlining what induction activities have happened should not be ticked and she should word her comment on the assessment form carefully. Perhaps something like this would be appropriate:

> I agree with my report. My progress has been hampered by the lack of support that my induction tutor has been able to give me because of her other duties. I have only had a reduced timetable in the weeks of .... I hope that next term I will get release time

regularly in order to observe and learn from other colleagues and make progress in developing my teaching.

Problem 3

Is there anything I can do to let the LA know my situation without dropping my school in it?

Professionally worded comments on the assessment form and phone calls to the person in charge of NQTs at the LA should be made. What you mustn't do is allow your development to suffer – or to risk failing. You are a professional and are expected to speak up for yourself in resolving issues.

Problem 4

Despite the improvements I have made in my classroom management, I have been informed by my induction mentor that I am not making satisfactory progress. I have failed on this area and also because my marking is not up to standard. My HOF told me about the marking two weeks ago and I have been working on it since (prioritising it ahead of planning). My mentor looked at two sets of books, one set was marked well, the other set (a class I struggle to get any work from) was unacceptable. I've only taught them 3 times since and they were preparing for and doing a test in that time. What I need to know is: what should I be writing in the box for my comments?

It really isn't the end of the world to not be deemed to be making satisfactory progress in the first term. I know someone who failed her first term with flying colours and a year later she is stunning and has become a really good induction tutor. In the comment box this NQT should write that he is making progress on marking and whether he agrees with the report as a whole. People should say what support they think they need (and have/have not had in the first term) in order to make clear progress against clear objectives. They should contact the LA, let them know if there have been any contraventions of the induction entitlement and ask whether there is any extra help. For instance, in many areas NQTs can have an advanced skills teacher (AST) work with them once a week – it really helps!

Problem 5

I'm currently off work with the 'flu and have not yet had an assessment meeting with my tutor – although I have been told that I have passed the first term. What happens about the forms that need to be filled in and sent off to the LA? Is there a deadline? Will my first term count?

The weeks before the end of term get very frenetic and people get ill. Since this can be predicted, it's a good idea to be proactive in getting a date for the meeting set before the end of term, so that there is time for it to be rescheduled if necessary. If you or the induction tutor are ill and the meeting doesn't happen or the report doesn't get written, it's not the end of the world. The term will still count towards your induction period. Someone should contact the LA and let them know that the report will be delayed. You'll need to make sure your assessment report and meeting are at the top of the agenda at the start of the new term, so that your progress is not delayed.

The assessment process should leave you confident in knowing your strengths, successes and next steps. This should set you up well for the rest of your career – your early and continuing professional development.

Bibliography

Bubb, S. (2007) *Successful Induction for New Teachers*. London: Sage.

Bubb, S., Earley, P. and Totterdell, M. (2005) 'Accountability and responsibility: 'Rogue' school leaders and the induction of new teachers in England', *The Oxford Review of Education* Vol. 31, No. 2, pp. 251–268.

Bubb, S., Heilbronn, R., Jones, C., Totterdell, M. and Bailey, M. (2002) *Improving Induction: Research Based Best Practice*. London: RoutledgeFalmer.

Department for Children, Families and Schools (2007) *The Standards' Framework*. London: DCSF.

Department for Children, Families and Schools (2008) *Statutory Guidance on Induction for Newly Qualified Teachers in England*. London: DCSF. www.teachernet.gov.uk/_doc/12703/080623%20 Induction%20Statutory%20Guidance.pdf.

Department for Children, Families and Schools (2009) *School Teachers' Pay and Conditions*. London: DCFS.

Department for Education and Skills (2003) *Raising Standards and Tackling Workload: A National Agreement*. London: DfES.

Earley, P. and Kinder, K. (1994) *Initiation Rights: Effective Induction Practices for New Teachers*. Slough: NFER.

Furlong, J. and Maynard, T. (1995) *Mentoring Student Teachers: A Practical Guide*. London: Falmer Press.

General Teaching Council for Scotland (2009) *The Standard for Full Registration*. Edinburgh: GTCS.

Graduate Teacher Training Registry (2008) *Annual Statistical Report*. Cheltenham: UCAS.

Howson, J. (2009) 'Job hot spots', *Times Educational Supplement*, First Appointments, January, p. 6.

Totterdell, M., Heilbronn, R., Bubb, S. and Jones, C. (2002) *Evaluation of the Effectiveness of the Statutory Arrangements for the Induction of Newly Qualified Teachers*. Research report no. 338. London: DCSF.

Training and Development Agency for Schools (2007) *Able to Teach.* London: TDA.

Training and Development Agency for Schools (2008a) *Professional Standards for Qualified Teacher Status and Requirements for Initial Teacher Training.* London: TDA. www.tda.gov.uk/partners/itt-standards/guidance_08/qts/Q01.aspx.

Training and Development Agency for Schools (2008b) *Results of the Newly Qualified Teacher Survey 2008.* London: TDA.

Training and Development Agency for Schools (2008c) *Annual Report 2007–08.* London: TDA.

Welsh Assembly Government (2009) *Induction and Early Professional Development.* Cardiff: WAG.

Index

action plan   140–3
appropriate body   126, 128–9,
    160–1
assessment (induction)   113,
    124–6, 129, 135–6, 157–65

BEd   6–7, 76, 123
being observed   56–60, 152–6
bursary   7, 10

contracts   101–2
CRB   24

display   69, 91, 110–11, 113

failing induction   160–1

GTP   6, 7, 9–11, 76, 123

induction programme   143–8
induction rules   124–7
induction tutor   123–4, 128,
    133–8
interview   16–19, 96–101

job hunting   87–9

lesson plans   45–8
literacy test   33–7

managing behaviour   51–4
marking   49–51, 86
MTL   11, 78

numeracy test   31–3

objectives   141–3
observing others   14–16, 146,
    148–52
Ofsted   6, 90, 153
overseas trained teachers   12–13

parents   54, 82, 115–19
pay   78, 87, 104–5
personal statement   93–6
PGCE   7–11, 75, 123
planning   45–9, 58, 112
pools   88–9
portfolio   139–41
PPA   108

reduced timetable   126, 129,
    145–8
references, referees (jobs)   14,
    92–3, 140
references, referencing
    (essays)   41–4
reports (pupils)   119–21, 138
roles and responsibilities
    (induction)   128–38
RTP   7, 76, 123

salary   104–5
Scotland   75–6, 122–4, 162
SEN   32, 108, 146–7
skills tests   13, 28–39
special schools   85
standards   25–7, 45, 59
stress   62–3, 122
study skills   40–1
supply teaching   82–4, 104

support staff   69, 112–15

Teacher Support Network   63
Teachers TV   46, 111, 118
teaching assistant   112–15
time management   67–71

unreasonable demands   130–2

voice   64–6

Wales   6, 9, 10, 75, 78, 122–4
workload   67, 69–70